More
New Testament
Studies

C H Dodd

Professor Emeritus in the
University of Cambridge

More
New Testament
Studies

Manchester University Press

Published by the
University of Manchester at
The University Press
316–324, Oxford Road
Manchester 13

GB SBN 7190 0333 4

Made and Printed in Great Britain by
Butler & Tanner Ltd, Frome and London

Preface

In 1953 the Manchester University Press published a collection of papers under the title, *New Testament Studies* (a title subsequently appropriated to the journal of the *Studiorum Novi Testamenti Societas*). I have here collected a further batch of papers, produced (with one exception) during the period from 1953.

No. 1 was first published in *Mélanges Bibliques rédigés en l'honneur de André Robert* (Bloud & Gay, Paris, 1955). No. 2 was published in *New Testament Essays: Studies in Memory of T. W. Manson* (Manchester University Press, 1959). Nos. 3 and 4 appeared, in a French translation, in special issues of the Strasbourg *Revue d'Histoire et de Philosophie religieuses* presented, respectively, to H. Clavier (1962) and J. Héring (1957). No. 5 was published in *Neotestamentica et Patristica: eine Freundesgabe Herrn Professor Oscar Cullmann überreicht* (Brill, Leiden, 1962). No. 6 appeared among papers presented to N. H. Baynes in the *Journal of Roman Studies*, 1947. No. 8 was published in *Studies in the Gospels: Essays in Memory of R. H. Lightfoot* (Blackwell, 1957). No. 9 was published in *Studia Paulina, in honorem Johannis de Zwaan* (Bohn, Haarlem, 1953). My thanks are due to the several publishers for their courteous permission to reprint these essays and articles. No. 7 is a slightly expanded lecture hitherto unpublished.

No. 2 has been partly re-written, with additional matter. Elsewhere revision has been slight.

Contents

		Page
	Preface	v
1	The Beatitudes: a form-critical study	1
2	The 'Primitive Catechism' and the Sayings of Jesus	11
3	A Hidden Parable in the Fourth Gospel	30
4	Behind a Johannine Dialogue	41
5	The Prophecy of Caiaphas: John xi. 47–53	58
6	The Fall of Jerusalem and the 'Abomination of Desolation'	69
7	The Historical Problem of the Death of Jesus	84
8	The Appearances of the Risen Christ: a study in form-criticism of the Gospels	102
9	Ἔννομος Χριστοῦ	134
I	Index Nominum	149
II	Index Locorum	151

1 The Beatitudes: a form-critical study

An exponent of medieval French literature, discussing the difficulties which beset textual criticism where oral tradition has played an important part, refers in one place to 'une très longue série de chansons... qui nous sont parvenues en trois ou en quatre rédactions a peu près contemporaines, *continument dissemblables, continument identiques*'.[1] His language might be applied, with but little exaggeration, to the two forms in which the Beatitudes have come down to us. The First and Third Gospels, if not contemporaneous, cannot be separated by any long lapse of time. In both the *pericopé* of the Beatitudes is the exordium to the Great Sermon, and the Matthaean and Lucan passages are in some sort identical, and yet at almost every point they are dissimilar. This combination of identity and dissimilarity meets us constantly in the Synoptic Gospels, but nowhere in a more striking or problematical way than here. The two forms, therefore, of the *pericopé* merit repeated comparative examination.

It will be well to start by defining the precise limits of the *pericopé* with which we are dealing, in its two forms.

In Matt. v. 3–12 we have a series of nine sayings beginning with the word μακάριοι. The first eight of these are of identical pattern. The makarism is in the third person and is followed by a ὅτι-clause giving the ground on which the makarism is pronounced. Each clause is extremely concise, and in each of these eight sayings the two clauses are rhythmically balanced.

The ninth is different. The makarism is in the second person plural. Instead of the extreme brevity which characterizes the others, there is a striking fulness of detail in the clause describing the condition of those who are pronounced blessed. It is directly followed, not by a ὅτι-clause giving the ground of

---

[1] J. Bédier, in *Histoire de la Nation française*, tome XII (*Historie des Lettres*, vol. I), p. 232, quoted by H. J. Chaytor, in *From Script to Print*, p. 118. My italics.

blessedness, but by what is virtually a repetition of the makarism in another form: χαίρετε καὶ ἀγαλλιᾶσθε. Then at last
we have the ὅτι-clause, and this is supported and elaborated
by an additional γὰρ-clause, containing a further reason why
the persons mentioned are declared to be blessed.
Formally, therefore, this ninth beatitude offers at every point
a contrast to the others. We may best regard verses 11–12 as a
transition to the next following section of the Sermon, consisting of three sayings addressed directly to the disciples in
the second person, and characterizing them as the persecuted
(11–12), as the salt of the earth (13), and as the light of the
world (14–16).

It would appear therefore that the ninth beatitude was not
conceived by the evangelist as an integral part of the series,
which is indeed marked as a complete unit by the repetition,
after the eighth makarism, of the same clause as that which
followed the first: ὅτι αὐτῶν ἐστιν ἡ βασιλεία τῶν οὐρανῶν. This
repetition effectively clamps the whole sequence together.
If, with many critics, we regard the makarism of the πραεῖς,
an adaptation of Ps. xxxvi. 11,[1] which has no constant position
in the MS tradition,[2] as a later addition, we should have a compact series of seven beatitudes, and this would be in harmony
with this evangelist's apparent predilection for the number
seven. In any case we shall be justified in considering the
pericopé of the beatitudes in its Matthaean form as consisting of the series of seven or eight, which begins with the
makarism of the πτωχοὶ τῷ πνεύματι and ends with that of the
persecuted.

In Lk. vi. 21–3 the Great Sermon opens, as in Matthew, with
a series of sayings each beginning with the word μακάριοι.
Unlike the Matthaean makarisms, the Lucan are all in the
second person plural. Otherwise, the first three follow much
the same pattern as the Matthaean seven (or eight). The fourth,

---

[1] References to the Old Testament are given according to Swete,
The Old Testament in Greek, Cambridge University Press.

[2] The makarism of the πραεῖς is the second of the series in D 33,
supported by many Old Latin MSS and by the Curetonian Syriac.
The majority of MSS and versions give it the third place.

on the other hand, resembles in form not the closing beatitude of the Matthaean seven (or eight), to which in meaning it is akin, but the supernumerary beatitude which we have proposed to connect with the two following sayings to constitute the second complete section[1] of the Sermon. The effect of Luke's treatment is already to give a markedly different complexion to the *pericopé*.

But we cannot stop here. In Luke the four beatitudes are immediately followed by four 'woes', which balance the beatitudes so closely that we cannot doubt that the evangelist intended beatitudes and woes to form a single whole. The blessedness of the poor, hungry, sorrowful and outcast is contrasted with the unhappy prospects of the rich, well fed, jovial and popular, and the contrast illumines, or even determines, the sense in which beatitudes and woes alike are to be understood.

This antithetical scheme is by no means peculiar to the Third Gospel. It has substantial Old Testament precedents. In the LXX the word μακάριος always represents the Hebrew אַשְׁרֵי. An alternative mode of expression is טוֹב ל ?, which hardly differs in meaning.[2] Makarisms in the one form or the other are common enough; and so are pronouncements in a contrary sense, where οὐαί stands for הוֹי, אִי, אוֹי. But it is those places where the two are combined to form a rhetorically effective antithesis that interest us at present.

Isaiah iii. 10-11 offers an early and classical example:

Say to the righteous that it is well with him (כִּי טוֹב)
For they shall eat the fruit of their doings.
Woe to the wicked; it is ill with him (אוֹי לְרָשָׁע רַע)
For the reward of his hands shall be given him.[3]

Here the LXX differs from the Hebrew, and apparently

---

[1] The other sayings comprised in this section, or sayings closely akin to them, occur in Luke in remote contexts, xiv. 34-5; xi. 33.

[2] Similarly the μαχάριοι οἱ . . . of the gospels appears as *tūbayhūn* in the Syriac versions.

[3] Neither the text nor the construction of the passage is quite certain, but the general sense is hardly in doubt.

translates a different text.[1] Consequently the resemblance to the gospel beatitudes does not appear in the Greek.

In Eccl. x. 16–17 we have the pair, μακαρία (אַשְׁרֵי) and οὐαί (אִי), just as in Luke:

> Woe to thee, land, whose king is a servant,
> And thy princes eat early in the morning!
> Blessed art thou, land, whose king is the son of a freeman,
> And thy princes eat in due season
> For strength and not for drunkenness!

For a similar antithesis, cf. Eccl. viii. 12–13, where the contrasted conditions of the pious and the impious are denoted by the expressions יְהֶה טוֹב לְ ... טוֹב לֹא־יְהֶה לְ ? ... In Tob. xiii. 12 (16), 14 (18), μακάριος is accompanied by εὐλογημένος, and the antithesis to both is ἐπικατάρατος.

The convention passes over into rabbinic usage. Thus in *Berachoth* 61 b, we have 'Blessed art thou (אשריך) Aqiba, because thou wast arrested for words of Torah; woe to thee (אוי לך) Pappos, because thou wast arrested for idle words'. A Greek equivalent would use μακάριος and οὐαί, as in Luke. In *Yoma* 87 a, the alternative expression טוֹב לְ is used, with אוי לְ as antithesis: 'Blessed are the righteous: not only do they have merit, but they acquire merit also for their children and their children's children to the end of all generations; woe to the ungodly: not only do they bring guilt upon themselves; they cause guilt to their children and their children's children to the end of all generations.'

These parallels may suffice to show that the Lucan beatitudes and woes, forming a unitary whole, are composed on a well-established literary pattern. The close correspondence of beatitude and woe is to be observed in the two rabbinic sayings and in Eccl. x. 16–17 no less than in the gospel.

So much for the mere form. We now turn to the content. The balanced makarisms and woes announce an impending reversal of conditions, or περιπέτεια. Those who are now poor, hungry, sorrowful and outcast will possess the Kingdom of

---

[1] LXX δήσωμεν for Hebrew אָמְרוּ looks as if the radicals אמר had been mistaken for אסר, but the corruption probably lies deeper.

God, and in doing so will have abundance of food, will laugh for joy and will receive a heavenly reward. On the contrary, these who are now rich, well fed, jovial and popular will lose their advantages. The rich have already received all the comfort they are to get (ἀπέχετε τὴν παράκλησιν ὑμῶν, cf. Matt. vi. 5), the well fed will go hungry and the jovial will mourn; the trouble that awaits the popular is left indefinite: their lot is that of the ψευδοπροφῆται.

It has often been observed that this dichotomy of rich and poor, with the promise of a reversal of conditions, is prominent elsewhere in the Third Gospel. It is a main theme of the Magnificat, where the πεινῶντες are to be satisfied with good things and the rich sent empty away (Lk. ii. 53). The parable of Dives and Lazarus (Lk. xvi. 19-31), again, might serve as a graphic illustration of the great reversal as it is described both in the Magnificat and in the *pericope* of beatitudes and woes. There are notable parallels of language (not only πλούσιος and πτωχός, but also χορτασθῆναι, ἀπέλαβες τὰ ἀγαθά, παρακαλεῖται), although the rhetorical form is of course quite different.

But it is not only in the Third Gospel that this *motif* occurs. In the Epistle of James there is the same stark contrast of the present state and future destiny of rich and poor. The poor are chosen by God as heirs of His kingdom (ii. 5); the rich are to mourn and weep (κλαύσατε, v. 1) for the miseries that are coming upon them; their laughter will be turned into mourning (γέλως εἰς πένθος, iv. 9). Once again, though the rhetorical form is widely different from that of the gospel *pericope*, the coincidences of language are striking. But the point to be noted is that these parts of the epistle, like the gospel *pericope*, reflect a well marked attitude or frame of mind, characterized by an acute sense of the miseries of an oppressed class, and by the expectation of a περιπέτεια.

All this has its setting in the secular thought of the time. Arnold Toynbee, in *A Study of History*, vol. IV, pp. 245-61, has discussed the importance of the conception of περιπέτεια in the changing Hellenistic society, and has shown how the early Christian expectation of a reversal of conditions and rôles has its place in this wider context. On the face of it, the Lucan *pericope* might appear to contemplate a catastrophic

revolution in which the proletariate achieves a signal success
at the expense of the privileged class. As such, it would fit into
a contemporary pattern of thought in the Hellenistic world.
But it is clear that it is a sublimated or 'etherialized' kind of
περιπέτεια that is here in view: the reward is ἐν οὐρανῷ, and
that clause conditions all the rest. If the parable of Dives and
Lazarus is allowed as an illustration, the 'etherialized' character
of the reversal of conditions is emphasized. It remains, however, that the Lucan *pericopé* of beatitudes and woes is conceived within the framework of an idea of περιπέτεια which
was familiar at the time.

The Matthaean *pericopé*, to which we now return, clearly does
not fall within this order of ideas at all. To begin with, the
mere absence of a list of 'woes' corresponding to the makarisms
gives it a decisively different stamp. Further, the regular
rhythm, recalling the established rhythms of Hebrew poetry,[1]
sustained through seven (or eight) verses, produces an effect
contrasting markedly with that of Luke's varied or irregular
rhythms. While the Lucan *pericopé* is no more than rhetorical
prose, the Matthaean has the effect of a poem or hymn in
seven (or eight) strophes. It somewhat resembles some of the
psalms of the Old Testament, particularly those which contain
makarisms, e.g. Ps. i; xxxi. 1–2; xl. 2–3; lxiv. 5; lxxxiii. 5–6. 12;
lxxxviii. 16–17; cxi. (the whole of this psalm being an expansion
of a single makarism); cxviii. 1–2; cxxvii. 1–4; cxlv. 5–7 (note,
διδόντα τροφὴν τοῖς πεινῶσιν). It is true that in the Old Testament we do not find a prolonged series of makarisms with
the word μακάριος constantly repeated. At most, the actual

[1] C. F. Burney, *The Poetry of our Lord*, p. 166 sqq. attempts to
reconstruct the presumed Aramaic original underlying the canonical
text, and concludes: 'The Beatitudes according to Matthew's version
exhibit clear indications of composition in rhyme and (in the main)
three-stress rhythm.' He is however obliged, in the interests of
rhythm, and rhyme, not only to omit πνεύματι in verse 3 and τὴν
δικαιοσύνην in verse 6, but also to emend verse 10. Yet even if some
irregularities in the rhythm are accepted, the generally poetical character of the *pericopé* is not lost. Burney is certainly right in saying that
verses 11–12, in contrast, have no such traits of verse composition.

word occurs twice in one context. But the description of the persons deserving of such makarisms, in passages of verse sometimes running to several strophes, has some real resemblance to the Matthaean *pericopé*. The latter, again, finds a certain analogy in a passage in the Wisdom of Jesus son of Sirach (xxv. 7–11), where the author pronounces blessed (ἐμακάρισα) ten types of human lot—the man who has an intelligent wife, who takes delight in his children, who sees the defeat of his enemies, who finds wisdom, and so forth. Although the actual formula μακάριος ὁ δεῖνα, occurs only twice, in effect we have a sequence of ten makarisms, like the sequence of seven (or eight) in the gospel. But whereas the list in Matthew is clamped into a unity by the repetition of the clause αὐτῶν ἐστιν ἡ βασιλεία τῶν οὐρανῶν, indicating that all the several kinds of blessedness are aspects of the one supreme blessing of possessing the Kingdom of Heaven, the list in Sirach moves to a climax: various types of men are indeed blessed, but their blessedness is as nothing compared to that of the man who fears the Lord. The ethos of the two passages is clearly different. Nevertheless Matthew and the son of Sirach are composing within the same literary *genre*.

But we have already passed beyond considerations of mere form, and it is time to ask, What is the real character and intention of the Matthaean beatitudes? In Luke the answer to this question was simple: there is to be a reversal of conditions and rôles, and even though it is a highly 'etherialized' kind of περιπέτεια, yet the poor, hungry, sorrowful and outcast will be such no longer, any more than the prosperous will retain their advantages. But in Matthew it is clear that some at least of the makarisms carry no sort of implication of any such change. The merciful will not cease to be merciful in receiving mercy. The pure in heart will not be less so because they see God. The peace-makers will not be any the less peace-makers in becoming sons of God. In these cases at least the makarisms depict (like some of the psalms cited above) types of character which have God's approval, and it is there, essentially, that their blessedness lies, even though different aspects of the divine approval are represented in terms of the 'eschatological' blessings of the Kingdom of Heaven. These makarisms give so strong an ethical colouring to the whole *pericopé* that the mind inevitably tends toward an ethical understanding of the others. Luke, for example, speaks of the doleful fate of those who are outcast for the sake of Christ in a context which tends to assimilate it to the troubles of those who are the victims of untoward conditions—who are poor, hungry, and sorrowful *simpliciter*, without any explicit reference to ideal motives. But the curt Matthaean form, μακάριοι οἱ δεδιωγμένοι ἕνεκεν δικαιοσύνης, brings exclusively into relief the ethical quality of the martyr's sufferings. Similarly, in this setting it would be natural to understand the 'mourners' in a sense analogous to that of Tob. xiii. 14: μακάριοι ὅσοι ἐλυπήθησαν ἐπὶ ταῖς μάστιξίν σου (*scil.* those of 'Jerusalem the Holy City', xiii. 9); to understand the πτωχοί as the pious and humble poor of many Old Testament passages; and to understand the hunger and thirst as the divine discontent which craves supernatural satisfactions (cf. Ps. xli. 4, Ecclus. xxiv. 21, etc.), even if the addition of the explanatory terms τῷ πνεύματι, τὴν δικαιοσύνην, be regarded (with many critics) as additions by the evangelist. It is true that the blessings assured to the various types all have 'eschatological' associations, or, to use language nearer to that of the gospels, are functions of the Kingdom of Heaven, or of God. They are thus fittingly bound together by the repeated assurance, αὐτῶν ἐστιν ἡ βασιλεία τῶν οὐρανῶν. But all would be entirely consistent with the idea of a kingdom which already ἔφθασεν ἐφ᾽ ὑμᾶς (Matt. xii. 28)—and after all, ἐστιν is in the present tense. Any idea of a kingdom yet to come by way of a catastrophic περιπέτεια is in the background.

Enough has perhaps been said to make the point that in the First and Third Gospels the *pericopé* of the Beatitudes has taken differing forms, each of which is a distinct and characteristic literary product, related to different established forms of composition, and that, in spite of the large common element which they share, each stands on its own proper footing. Full justice should be done to this fact before criticism attempts to trace the pre-canonical history of the Beatitudes, whether by way of literary dependence on sources or by way of development in oral tradition. It may at any rate be said that if either evangelist be supposed to depend on the other, or both upon some hypothetical source, something much more radical than a mere 'editing' of borrowed material is to be taken into account. Nor is the question, which of the two is the more 'primitive', or the more 'authentic', in the sense of representing more exactly the actual wording of the Beatitudes as they were originally spoken, so simple a question as it has sometimes been made to appear. No doubt some probabilities may be established by minute analysis and comparison, but perhaps we can with confidence say little more than that when the tradition emerges into our ken, the Beatitudes had already taken two diverse forms[1] represented by Matthew and Luke respectively. In that sense both are 'primitive'. But whether these traditional forms

[1] Here again I may adduce a further quotation from a passage dealing with partly similar phenomena in a different field, that of the traditional poetry of the Middle Ages. Pio Rajna, *Ricerche intorno ai Reali di Francia*, p. 144, is discussing the transmission of the Story of Buove (*anglice*, Bevis of Hamptoun), of which two diverse recensions are extant. 'Nessuno dei due testi', he observes, 'si può tenere trascrizione di quello che trasportò premieramente in Italia la storia di Buove, sibbene entrambi furono composti dietro reminiscenze, sicchè ora l'uno ora l'altro riusci più fedele . . . Di tempo in tempo qualche verso, qualche parola nei due testi si accorda, mentre solitamente la forma differisce al tutto, togliendo cosi ogni ragione di sospettare che l'uno dei due autori scrivesse tenendo sotto gli occhi l'opera del altro. Quale delle due versioni sia stata composta la prima, non saprei dire: ambedue credo s'abbiano a collocare tra il 1250 e il 1330' (quoted by Chaytor, *op. cit.*, p. 125). Some of this language, it seems, might be applied *mutatis mutandis*, to our present problem. The *mutanda* certainly are considerable. The conditions of the problem are too different for principles of judgment to be transferred directly from the field of medieval literature to that of early Christianity; for one thing, in the latter field the lapse of time is so much shorter between the original creation of the material and its emergence in literature; for another thing, the community in which transmission took place was more closely knit. Yet where oral transmission played so large a part, *some* of the conditions are analogous.

B

reflect distinct modes of presentation adopted by the Lord himself on different occasions, or whether they developed in the course of giving shape to the Church's recollections of his teaching, is a question more difficult to answer.

2 The 'Primitive Catechism' and the Sayings of Jesus

That the first generation of the Christian Church retained some effective memory of the sayings of its Founder, and that this served as basis for a developing tradition which ultimately entered into our gospels, would seems a reasonable assumption, though it cannot be proved—or disproved. If so, then the critical study of the gospels, over and above any illumination it may bring to phases of Christian life and thought in the obscure earliest period of church history, may legitimately aim at working back, through the recovery of the underlying tradition, to a point as near as we can hope to get to what Jesus actually said. This purpose may be served by the attempt to identify, as far as possible, the channels through which the sayings may have been transmitted, in order to estimate the extent to which the accuracy of the report may be trusted, or, on the other hand, its content may have been subject to modifying influences.

There has in recent years been much inquisition after such channels of transmission, especially with the aid of the methods of form-criticism, and not without valuable results; but it may be worth while going over some of the ground once more.

It is natural to assume that the sayings of Jesus were recalled to serve the purpose of instruction in the principles of Christian belief and practice. Indeed, that is perhaps a glimpse of the obvious. In itself it does not get us very far, for our direct knowledge of methods of instruction in the early Church is limited, and the argument does not always avoid the danger of slipping into a circle. In one department, however, I think we may now say that we have at any rate a little solid knowledge: I mean the elementary instruction given to candidates for admission to the Church as preparation for their baptism, commonly described as *catechesis*. I would refer in particular to the work of Archbishop Carrington[1] and the late

[1] P. Carrington, *The Primitive Christian Catechism* (C.U.P. 1940).

E. G. Selwyn[1] on catechetical material in the Epistles. They
have, I believe, laid down lines on which it is possible to en-
visage what the former calls the Primitive Christian Catechism—
fragmentarily, no doubt, but as something that one can work
with. In order to do so it is not necessary to accept all the
details of their ingenious reconstructions. But I believe we are
entitled to assume that forms of teaching of the kind envisaged
were traditional during the New Testament period.

We have evidence for the beginnings, at any rate, of some
traditional scheme of teaching at a very early date. Already in
what is probably the earliest extant Christian document,
Paul's First Epistle to the Thessalonians, we find references to
a 'tradition' (ii. 13, iv. 1–8; cf. II Thess. ii. 15, iii. 6) which the
recipients of the letter had received from the apostles. As they
were Christians of no more than a few weeks' standing, we
may take it that the writer is recalling teaching which he had
given either as *catechesis* in the strict sense, or at any rate
as elementary instruction for new converts. The following
topics are either expressly stated or necessarily implied to have
formed part of this fundamental instruction: (i) theological
dogmas: monotheism and the repudiation of idolatry; Jesus
the Son of God; his resurrection and second advent; salvation
from the Wrath (i. 9–10); the calling of the Church into the
kingdom and glory of God (ii. 12); (ii) ethical precepts
(παραγγελίαι, i.e. 'marching orders', iv. 2, 11, cf. II Thess.
iii. 6, 10, 12): the holiness of the Christian calling; repudiation
of pagan vices; the law of charity (iv. 3–9); eschatological
motives (v. 2).

So much is clearly the minimum content of the παράδοσις.
That it actually contained more than this there can be little
doubt. In particular, the injunctions regarding church order
and discipline in v. 12–22 are given with an allusive brevity
which would be more in place in recalling maxims already
familiar than in breaking fresh ground. In II Thess. iii. 7–10
similar injunctions are expressly said to have been given
previously (τὴν παράδοσιν ἣν παρελάβετε . . . ὅτε ἦμεν πρὸς

---

[1] E. G. Selwyn, *The First Epistle of St. Peter* (Macmillan, 1946), pp.
363–466.

ὑμᾶς τοῦτο παρηγγέλλομεν ὑμῖν—note the imperfect tense of continuous or habitual action).[1] And it is noteworthy that under this head the mutual duties of members of the Church expand into universal social duties (πάντοτε τὸ ἀγαθὸν διώκετε εἰς ἀλλήλους καὶ εἰς πάντας, I Thess. v. 15), which may have been specified in the actual teaching. Similarly, we must suppose that a good deal of the eschatological *paraenesis* in v. 3–10 comes under the rubric, ἀκριβῶς οἴδατε, although these words apply directly only to the content of v. 2.

We see already emerging a 'pattern of teaching' (τύπος διδαχῆς, Rom. vi. 17), the general lines of which appear in other epistles. Omitting for our present purpose the properly theological portions, we may set out the table of contents somewhat as follows:

A. The holiness of the Christian calling.

B. The repudiation of pagan vices, leading up to—

C. The assertion of the Christian law of charity (ἀγάπη, including φιλαδελφία).

D. Eschatological motives.

E. The order and discipline of the Church: duties of its members to one another [social duties at large].

These topics tend to reappear in combination in the 'ethical section' of various epistles. Even the long and comprehensive outline of Christian ethics in Rom. xii–xiii follows with little divergence the plan of the παραγγελίαι of I Thessalonians. Starting with the holiness of the Christian calling (A), here under the figure of sacrifice (xii. 1–2), the writer moves on to the theme of the unity of the Church and the functions of its members (E) (xii. 3–8); then comes a long section applying the law of charity (C) to Christian conduct within the community (φιλαδελφία, xii, 10–16) and to social duties in general (xii.

---

[1] I see no sufficient reason for rejecting the evidence of II Thessalonians. The objections to Pauline authorship have no great weight if we allow for the probability that in ii. 3–10 we have material drawn from some Christian prophecy. If, however, non-Pauline turns of phrase suggest a different authorship, Silvanus, after all, is named in the superscription even though it is Paul who signs at the end.

17–xiii. 7), and subsuming it all once again under the law of charity (xiii. 8–10); he then finishes with a section of eschatological *paraenesis* (D),[1] in terms closely similar in part to those of I Thess. v. 2–10. Only the section on the repudiation of pagan vices is missing, and this theme has been dismissed in ch. i.

It is not necessary here to trace the pattern in other epistles, where it has been amply studied. But it is noteworthy that it still underlies the detailed manual of instruction known as 'The Teaching of the Lord through the Twelve Apostles' (commonly referred to as *Didaché*). There is nothing indeed expressly corresponding with section A, on the holiness of the Christian calling, but the contrast between pagan vices and the Christian law of charity (B, C) is here, only in reverse order, in the passage on the Two Ways (i–vi). The familiar list of vices in v leaves no doubt where it belongs. There follows an elaborate section on church order and discipline (D), (vii–xv). It contains a great deal for which earlier examples of the

---

[1] In Romans the eschatological section concludes the catechetical material (for ch. xiv belongs to a different category). In I Thess., as we have seen, it precedes the section on church order. But in that epistle Paul had special reasons for including fresh teaching (οὐ θέλομεν ὑμᾶς ἀγνοεῖν, iv. 13) upon eschatology, and he has appended to it a reminder of teaching already known, before going on to Church order. In James, as in I Thess. a section of eschatological *paraenesis* (v. 7–9) precedes a passage relating to discipline and practice in the Church (v. 13–16). In I Peter there are two sequences of catechetical material; in the first, a brief piece of eschatological *paraenesis* (iv: 7) is sandwiched between the repudiation of pagan vices (iv. 3–6) and the affirmation of the law of ἀγάπη (iv. 8–9), which in turn is followed by a section on church order; in the second, the characteristic injunctions associated with eschatological *paraenesis* follow the section on church order, and virtually close the epistle (v. 6–9). In Ephesians the passage corresponding with the eschatological *paraenesis* forms the virtual close of the epistle (vi. 10–18). In the *Didaché* there is a full-scale eschatological section at the end. It is evident that, while the sequence of sections varies, the eschatological section tends to gravitate to the close of the *catechesis*.

τόπος διδαχῆς found no place, but in the less specialized sections familiar turns of phrase are frequent enough to arrest the attention of the reader who has earlier writings in mind. Finally we have a passage which combines apocalyptic prediction with *paraenesis* (D) in the traditional manner (xvi). The *Didaché* is to all appearance a highly composite document. Its date, and its relations with the gospels and other early Christian literature, are questions on which critical opinion is widely divergent. Its significance for our present purpose is as evidence for the persistence of a pattern of teaching once established. It is indeed the pattern itself which is the constant element. There is no sufficient evidence of a complete documentary catechism from which various writers might be supposed to quote. All that we are entitled to infer is a kind of programme or schedule of instruction, which could be filled in and expanded orally in various ways. Nevertheless, in passages which we may suppose to be following the established pattern we frequently discern a common style, and this style is often in contrast with the habitual style of the author concerned. We may take it to be the style of early Christian *catechesis*. It has analogues in the style of the Jewish Wisdom literature, and of documents like the *Testaments of the Twelve Patriarchs* and the *Manual of Discipline* from Qumran, and also in Jewish-Hellenistic propaganda-literature such as that of the pseudo-Phocylides. On the other side it has some resemblance to the style of Greek gnomic writers.[1] Agreeably with these indications from style we note that in form and often in content the early Christian *catechesis* has clear points of contact both with Jewish patterns of instruction used in the admission of proselytes,[2] on the one hand, and, on the other hand, with popular Stoic teaching. That is to say, it bears traces of precisely those influences which we should expect to have helped to mould the practice of the new community as it first grew up in a Jewish environment and then moved out into the

[1] See H. Chadwick, *The Sententiae of Sextus* (*Texts and Studies*, C.U.P. new series, no. 5), introduction.

[2] See D. Daube, 'A Baptismal Catechism', in *The N.T. and Rabbinic Judaism* (Athlone Press, 1956), pp. 106–40.

Graeco-Roman world, following largely in the tracks of Jewish-Hellenistic missionaries. If we are to conjecture a date for the more or less definite fixing of this pattern, we should be led, it seems, to the earliest period in which Greek-speaking converts from paganism began to enter the Church in such numbers that the need for a standardized *catechesis* became pressing. This period might perhaps begin with the rise of a gentile Christianity at Antioch, and, as we have seen, the ethical παϱάδοσις was already in existence at any rate by the time of Paul's visit to Thessalonica, A.D. 49. This is not to rule out the probability of other forms of *catechesis*, as early or earlier, more directly based on Jewish models, and less affected by Hellenistic influence. It is thought by many critics that some such slightly Christianized Jewish catechism underlies parts of the *Didaché*.

The way in which the content of these largely inherited forms was transformed by distinctively Christian motives I have tried to illustrate elsewhere.[1] The question before us here is a different one. Granted that we have a not inadequate general picture of the forms of catechetical instruction employed in the early Church during its formative period, can these be related to the teaching of Jesus as presented in the gospels in such a way that they may reasonably be regarded as a channel through which his sayings were transmitted during the period of oral tradition before the gospels were written?

The first general observation that occurs is that the pattern of teaching almost always includes a passage, which tends to be placed at the end, appealing to eschatological motives for Christian conduct, and that in the gospels eschatological *paraenesis* holds a similar place. In all three Synoptics the report of the teaching of Jesus closes with the Eschatological Discourse, which has its equivalent in portions of the Farewell Discourses in the Fourth Gospel.[2] It is a probable inference that the traditional order of *catechesis* determined, to this extent at least, the arrangement of didactic material in the gospels.

[1] In *Gospel and Law* (Columbia University Press and C.U.P. 1951), pp. 25–45.

[2] See C. H. Dodd, *The Interpretation of the Fourth Gospel* (C.U.P. 1953), pp. 390–6.

Moreover, traces of its influence are perhaps not confined to the composition of the gospels as a final product, but are to be found also in some of their constituent parts, which may point to earlier sources constructed on a similar plan.

The Great Sermon, in its Matthaean version, ends on an eschatological note. The reference in Matt. vii. 22 to ἐκείνη ἡ ἡμέρα makes it clear that this evangelist understood these sayings in an eschatological sense, and that he took the storm and floods of the parable of the Two Builders as symbols of the coming Judgment. With this clue, it is possible to suspect a wider influence of the general pattern in the structure of the Sermon as a whole. The Beatitudes, with the sayings immediately following (v. 3–16), may be regarded as an equivalent in some sort for the section on the holiness of the Christian calling (A). Then comes a long section in which, as in sections B and C, the new Christian way is contrasted with the old ways which the convert is leaving (v. 17–48). Like the *catechesis* of the epistles, it culminates in the statement of the Christian law of charity, but where the epistles contrast the Christian way with the vices of paganism, the Sermon points the contrast with the casuistry of scribal Judaism. The next section of the Sermon (vi. 1–18) deals with almsgiving, fasting and prayer (corporate prayer, since the model provided is in the first person plural), and this would readily fall into the section (E) about church order and discipline, to which also the saying about pearls before swine (vii. 6) and about false prophets (vii. 15–20) might reasonably be assigned. Both of these themes, as well as those of prayer and fasting, are integral parts of the corresponding section in the *Didaché* (viii–ix, xi. 3–5). The intervening sections of the Sermon fall outside the common pattern. It seems however not too rash to infer that the structure of the Sermon in its Matthaean version has been influenced at some stage by a form of catechetical instruction, if it is not based directly upon it. The Hellenistic element which we have noted in the epistles is absent from the Sermon. Whether the evangelist made use of a pre-existing catechism current in Jewish-Christian circles, or, being himself familiar with the pattern of teaching followed in such circles, organized his material on this pattern, the *catechesis* would seem to have provided a vehicle for part at least of the material comprised in the Sermon.

In the Lucan version of the Sermon it is much more difficult to discern traces of the catechetical scheme. Here the Beatitudes (with their balancing Woes) no longer have the character which they show in Matthew.[1] The Christian law of charity is stated but without the contrast with the old ways. The saying about the tree and its fruit (vi. 43–4) is given without the application to false prophets which it has in Matthew, and so loses its relevance to church discipline. The saying about those who say 'Lord, Lord' is given without its eschatological setting.[2] The parable of the Two Builders similarly has no expressly eschatological reference.

The Lucan version of the Sermon thus appears to retain little of the traditional form of *catechesis*. Yet some of the material embodied in the Matthaean Sermon occurs in a different context in Luke (xii. 22–34), where it leads up at once to a passage which has much in common with the Eschatological Discourse (xii. 35–46), as well as with the eschatological section (D) of the common form of *catechesis*. That we may have traces here of an earlier source (whether documentary or oral) which followed the traditional order of the *catechesis*, and ended with a piece of eschatological *paraenesis*, is a not unreasonable conjecture. If so, it has become disintegrated through combination with extraneous material.

We seem, then, to have found evidence that the catechetical scheme may have provided a kind of schedule, defining the order in which topics might be treated. We have still to ask how far the contents show significant points of similarity in language or substance. Here again we turn first to the eschatological section. The main burden of this section in the *catechesis* is the attitude and conduct demanded of the Christian in view of the fact that the End is near but its date uncertain: τὸ τέλος ἤγγικεν (I Pet. iv. 7), ἡ παρουσία τοῦ κυρίου ἤγγικεν (Jas. v. 8), ἡ ἡμέρα ἤγγικεν (Rom. xiii. 11), ἡμέρα κυρίου ὡς κλέπτης

[1] See above, pp. 2–6.
[2] Though the eschatological sayings associated with it in Matthew were known to Luke in another version, cf. xiii. 24–27.

ἔρχεται (I Thess. v. 2), and the like. The 'Day of the Lord' tends to be thought of as the dawn coming to end the night, and this brings in the antitheses of light and darkness, sleep and wakefulness, drunkenness and sobriety, which are found in Jewish contexts but are also especially beloved of Hellenistic moralists.[1] The recurrent key-words are ἐξ ὕπνου ἐγερθῆναι, γρηγορεῖν, ἀγρυπνεῖν, νήφειν, σωφρονεῖν, in James μακροθυμεῖν. A note of militancy is not far below the surface: in I Thess. v. 8 the call for wakefulness and sobriety suggests the armed Christian warrior; in Rom. xiii. 12, similarly, since dawn is at hand the Christian must put on τὰ ὅπλα τοῦ φωτός; in I Pet. v. 8-9 νήψατε, γρηγορήσατε is followed by the call to resist (ἀντιστῆναι) the devil, 'armed', perhaps, with the mind of Christ (τὴν αὐτὴν ἔννοιαν ὁπλίσασθε, iv. 1). In I Pet. iv. 7 the idea of wakefulness or sobriety in view of the nearness of the End is specifically associated with prayer: πάντων δὲ τὸ τέλος ἤγγικεν· σωφρονήσατε οὖν καὶ νήψατε εἰς προσευχάς. In Ephesians, where explicit eschatology is only faintly present, the whole of the eschatological *paraenesis* is reduced to an eloquent passage upon the Christian warfare against the powers of darkness (vi. 10-17). The picture of the Christian warrior equipped with the πανοπλία τοῦ θεοῦ is reminiscent of the strongly eschatological passage in I Thess. v. 7-9, but more elaborate. The exhortation to sleepless vigilance, which is in itself entirely germane to the military imagery, is here, as in I Pet. iv. 7, associated with prayer: προσευχόμενοι ἐν παντὶ καιρῷ ἐν πνεύματι καὶ εἰς αὐτὸ ἀγρυπνοῦντες ἐν πάσῃ προσκαρτερήσει (vi. 18). In the corresponding passage of Colossians (iv. 2-3) the exhortation to perseverance and wakefulness is again associated with prayer, but it has lost even its vestigial connection with eschatology. It is perhaps significant that when all the rest of the eschatological *paraenesis* has faded out, γρηγορεῖτε, ἀγρυπνεῖτε remains as its permanent legacy to the Christian moral ideal.

We now turn to the gospels, and primarily to the Eschatological Discourse which concludes the report of the teaching

---

[1] See C. H. Dodd, *The Bible and the Greeks* (Hodder & Stoughton, 1935), pp. 187-91.

of Jesus. The burden of the *paraenesis* here is closely similar to that of the eschatological section of the *catechesis*, and its style, though not identical, is sufficiently similar, and sufficiently unlike the prevailing style of some other parts of the gospels, to warrant the belief that some relation existed between them at any early stage in the formation of the tradition.

Here again the motive for conduct is found in the nearness of the End and the uncertainty of its date, which should lead the Christian to be wakeful and alert: ἐγγύς ἐστιν ἐπὶ θύραις . . . ἀγρυπνεῖτε, οὐκ οἴδατε γὰρ πότε ὁ καιρός ἐστιν . . . γρηγορεῖτε οὖν . . . πᾶσιν λέγω, γρηγορεῖτε (Mk. xiii. 29, 33, 37); γρηγορεῖτε οὖν ὅτι οὐκ οἴδατε τὴν ἡμέραν οὐδὲ τὴν ὥραν (Matt. xxv. 13); and the like. As the various forms of *catechesis* call for μακροθυμία under trial, and for 'armed' resistance in the spiritual conflict, so the Eschatological Discourse calls for ὑπομονή to the end (Mk. xiii. 13, Lk. xxi. 19).

In the Lucan form of the Discourse a passage (xxi. 34-6) is introduced which has a striking likeness to the language of eschatological *paraenesis* in the catechetical sections of the epistles, chiefly of I Thessalonians:

Προσέχετε δὲ ἑαυτοῖς
μήποτε βαρηθῶσιν ὑμων αἱ καρδίαι
ἐν κραιπάλῃ[1] καὶ μέθῃ καὶ μερίμναις βιωτικαῖς, Cf I Thess. v. 7
καὶ ἐπιστῇ ἐφ᾽ ὑμᾶς αἰφνίδιος ἡ ἡμέρα ἐκείνη . . .Cf. I Thess. v. 3
ἀγρυπνεῖτε δὲ ἐν παντὶ καιρῷ δεόμενοι . . .　　　Cf. Eph. vi. 18
　　　　　　　　　　　　　　　　　　　　　　　　I Pet. iv. 7
ἵνα κατίσχυσητε ἐκφυγεῖν ταῦτα πάντα . . .　　Cf. I Thess. v. 3
καὶ σταθῆναι ἔμπροσθεν τοῦ υἱοῦ τοῦ ἀνθρώπου　Cf. Eph. vi. 13

It is improbable that the evangelist was drawing upon the epistles for his material; but if he was (as I have suggested) following the general arrangement of a common form of *catechesis*, its language too may well have been in his mind. Here, then, we have good reason to suppose that the primitive catechism, in serving as a vehicle for transmitting the teaching of Jesus, has helped to mould the report of his sayings.

It is noteworthy that the language for the most part belongs

---

[1] *Corp. Herm* vii. 27; νήψατε παύσασθε κραιπαλῶντες, and see C. H. Dodd, *Parables of the Kingdom* (Nisbet 1961), p. 124.

more particularly to the Hellenistic strain in the early *catechesis*. But there is one feature which is not Hellenistic—the association of *prayer* with the wakefulness, stedfastness and endurance required of the Christian in view of the critical situation (ἀγρυπνεῖτε . . . ἐνδεόμενοι). In the catechetical section of the epistles this association recurs, as we have seen, in Ephesians, Colossians and I Peter. But it is far more impressively and memorably affirmed in a passage of the gospels which ostensibly does not belong to the record of the teaching of Jesus at all: Mk. xiv. 38, γρηγορεῖτε καὶ προσεύχεσθε. The passage is an integral part of the Passion narrative. Yet Mark was hardly unaware of its didactic value, or of its aptness to the theme of sleeping and waking in the *catechesis*. There is some probability in the suggestion that the Gethsemane *pericopé*, detached from its context in the Passion narrative, may have had a place of its own in Christian teaching, and that this may have affected the language of the passage. The sentence which follows upon the injunction to 'watch and pray', τὸ μὲν πνεῦμα πρόθυμον ἡ δὲ σὰρξ ἀσθενής, has been described as 'a fine piece of rhetorical prose, drawn perhaps from a Christian sermon'.[1] The style is not in Mark's customary vein. Obviously, nothing could have been employed to more profound effect to enforce the maxim, ἀγρυπνεῖτε, γρηγορεῖτε, than the story of the dismal collapse of the disciples who were asleep at the moment of destiny.

It looks, then, as if there had been some interaction between two distinct channels of tradition, the catechetical pattern on the one hand and the Passion narrative on the other. Priority here may be thought to belong to the latter. The association of prayer with wakefulness is hardly a standing feature of the catechetical scheme. The three epistles in which we have noted it—Ephesians, Colossians and I Peter—form a group with many common features quite apart from the catechetical pattern which they share.[2] On the other hand in Romans and

---

[1] W. L. Knox, *Sources of the Synoptic Gospels* (C.U.P. 1953), vol. I, p. 126.

[2] See C. L. Mitton, *The Epistle to the Ephesians* (Clar. Press 1951), pp. 176–97, for Ephesians and I Peter. The relation of Ephesians to Colossians is notoriously close, however it is to be explained.

I Thessalonians the exhortation to constant prayer (τῇ προσ-
ευχῇ προσκαρτεροῦντες, Rom. xii. 12, ἀδιαλείπτως προσεύχεσθε,
I Thess. v. 17) is detached from the eschatological *paraenesis*
and associated, in Romans with the general outline of Christian
virtues as manifestations of ἀγάπη, and in I Thessalonians with
prescriptions on church order and discipline. Similarly in the
Didaché the section beginning Γρηγορεῖτε (xvi. 1 sqq.) has
nothing on the theme of prayer, which comes in the section
dealing with church order and liturgy.[1] It would seem to be
consistent with the evidence if we said that the constant
emphasis, in the instructions given to converts, on the duty of
wakefulness helped to keep in memory this element in the
story of the Passion of the Lord, that while he prepared himself
by prayer for the approaching πειρασμός his disciples slept,
and were overtaken by it, and the remembrance of his words
to them, γρηγορεῖτε καὶ προσεύχεσθε, linked the idea of prayer
with the whole complex of wakefulness, stedfastness, forti-
tude with which this part of the *catechesis* was occupied. The
words were originally spoken in reference to the immediate
crisis of the betrayal and arrest of Jesus; they were now applied
to the expected crisis of his second advent, and in that sense
penetrated into the form of *catechesis* represented by Ephesians
and I Peter. But it is represented even more distinctly in
Lk. xxi. 34–6, where a development of the *catechesis* is fed
back into the record of the sayings of Jesus: προσέχετε
ἑαυτοῖς μήποτε. . . ἐπιστῇ ἐφ᾽ ὑμᾶς αἰφνίδιος ἡ ἡμέρα ἐκείνη ὡς
παγίς . . . ἀγρυπνεῖτε δεόμενοι. The disciples, in the story of
the Passion, did not keep awake or pray, and the Day did
come unexpectedly on them 'like a trap'. Luke's language,
deeply coloured (as we have seen) by Hellenistic influence, is
remote from that of the older tradition of the sayings of Jesus,
but a memory of Gethsemane lurks in thebackground.[2]

---

[1] If there is anything in the suggestion made above (pp. 17–18)
that part of the material in the Sermon on the Mount came down in
a catechetical framework, then, here again, the theme of prayer seems
to have been associated as in the *Didaché* with fasting and almsgiving without any eschatological context (Matt. vi. 2–17).

[2] In Luke's own account of Gethsemane the exhortation to wake-

For the further illustration of this apparent interaction of two strains of tradition we may turn again to the eschatological *paraenesis* of I Thess. v. 1–10. Here the unexpectedness of the End is expressed in the terms, ἡμέρα κυρίου ὡς κλέπτης ἐν νυκτὶ οὕτως ἔρχεται. The image fits in well with the sustained imagery of day and night, sleeping and waking, which pervades the passage. But it directly recalls a parable which occurs as part of the Eschatological Discourse in Matthew (xxiv. 43–4). In Luke (xii. 39) a slightly different version of the parable is found in a context which I have conjectured to represent the eschatological conclusion of a sequence derived from some earlier source (p. 18 above). In the Lucan form of the parable however, there is nothing about night or about wakefulness: εἰ ἤδει ὁ οἰκοδεσπότης ποίᾳ ὥρᾳ ὁ κλέπτης ἔρχεται, οὐκ ἂν ἀφῆκεν διορυχθῆναι τὸν οἶκον αὐτοῦ. So far as we are told, the raid might have taken place either by night or by day; ὥρα would serve for either. The householder may have been at fault, not in falling asleep, but in going from home without providing protection for his property. The moral is not, 'Keep awake', but simply, 'Be prepared': γίνεσθε ἕτοιμοι, ὅτι ᾗ ὥρᾳ οὐ δοκεῖτε ὁ υἱὸς τοῦ ἀνθρώπου ἔρχεται. This is the moral in Matthew, but in addition he has introduced the terms φυλακῇ (implying night) for ὥρᾳ, and ἐγρηγόρησεν ἄν, and so associated the parable with the *paraenesis* about night and day, sleeping and waking.

How are we to account for these phenomena? No one surely would seriously contend that the image of the thief who arrives unpredictably had its origin in the *catechesis* and that the parable was derived from it. In I Thessalonians the image is a passing simile (ὡς κλέπτης), one of a series of rhetorical figures running through the passage (ὥσπερ ἡ ὠδῖν ... ἐνδυσάμενοι θώρακα κ.τ.λ.). The parable on the contrary is a swift and vivid evocation of a situation in real life,[1] and this is characteristic

---

fulness is not present except as implied in τί καθεύδετε; but the words of xxi. 36, ἀγρυπνεῖτε δεόμενοι ἵνα κατισχύσητε ἐκφυγεῖν ταῦτα might almost be said to be a paraphrase of γρηγορεῖτε καὶ προσεύχεσθε ἵνα μὴ ἔλθητε εἰς πειρασμόν.

[1] Perhaps, as Jeremias suggests, a recent incident well known to

of the gospel parables as a whole, which bear the stamp of an individual mind, and are very generally allowed to be the most clearly self-authenticating element in the Sayings as handed down. A brief allusion to the parable would be natural enough for a teacher inculcating the lesson of wakeful preparedness for the unpredictable crisis ahead. It seems to follow that the parable was already known to the teacher at least, and possibly to his pupils.[1] It was therefore handed down by a channel of tradition independent of the *catechesis*, as was the Passion narrative in the last example. Once the figure of the thief had established itself in catechetical usage, its association there with night and the need for wakefulness acted upon the tradition of the parable, and so we arrive at the Matthaean version, where the parable is firmly embedded in a setting which is essentially that of the *catechesis*: γρηγορεῖτε οὖν, ὅτι οὐκ οἴδατε ποίᾳ ἡμέρᾳ ὁ κύριος ὑμῶν ἔρχεται. ἐκεῖνο δὲ γινώσκετε, ὅτι εἰ ᾔδει ὁ οἰκοδεσπότης ποίᾳ φυλακῇ ὁ κλέπτης ἔρχεται, ἐγρηγόρησεν ἄν. The most natural explanation of the curious interrelations of the three passages is that the image of the surprise visit of a thief, as a picturesque illustration of the folly of unpreparedness, came down both by way of the catechetical τύπος διδαχῆς and in a separate tradition of the parables of Jesus, and that there was reciprocal influence.

So far our examples have been drawn from the eschatological section of the *catechesis* and parts of the gospels which have affinity with it. In other sections it is less easy to define common ground on which the relations of different forms of tradition might be studied. But here and there it seems possible to detect indications of some kind of interaction.

One of the surest pointers to catechetical material is the

---

his auditors: *einen unlängst erfolgten Einbruch, von dem das ganze Dorf redet* (*Die Gleichnisse Jesu*, 1962, pp. 45–46).

[1] Ἀκριβῶς οἴδατε (v. 2) might be taken to refer to their acquaintance with the tradition of the Sayings, as θεοδίδακτοι in iv. 9 might refer to knowledge of the Scriptures (ἀγαπήσεις τὸν πλησίον) or, alternatively to the 'new commandment' of Christ as we have it in the Fourth Gospel. But it may refer to the catechetical instruction they had received.

occurrence of the stereotyped lists of vices, which Christian moralists inherited from their Hellenistic (and Hellenistic-Jewish) predecessors.[1] It was surely from this source that Mark drew the exegetical comment which he has appended to a saying of Jesus in vii. 16–23. Jesus has said, οὐδέν ἐστιν ἔξω τοῦ ἀνθρώπου εἰσπορευόμενον εἰς αὐτὸν ὃ δύναται κοινῶσαι αὐτόν ἀλλὰ τά ἐκ τοῦ ἀνθρώπου ἐκπορευόμενά ἐστιν τὰ κοινοῦντα τὸν ἄνθρωπον. The disciples are uncertain about the meaning of this saying (which is described as a παραβολή, no doubt in the more general sense of an enigmatic utterance) so they ask in private[2] for elucidation, which is given. The first member of the antithesis (εἰσπορευόμενον) is to be understood as referring to food (καθαρίζων πάντα τὰ βρώματα). The second member (ἐκπορευόμενα) is explained in terms of a conventional list of vices—πορνεῖαι, κλοπαί, φόνοι κ.τ.λ. We have reason to believe that this saying was discussed in the early Church,[3] and it may well have been brought into relation with that section of the *catechesis* (B in the analysis above, p. 13), which set forth the new outlook to which the convert was now committed, and in doing so pointed the contrast with the old ways he was abandoning, and left him in

[1] Cf. Rom. i. 29–31, I Cor. v. 11, vi. 9–10, Gal. v. 19–21, Eph. v. 3–5, Col. iii. 5–8, I Tim. i. 9–10, II Tim. iii. 2–4, etc. For instances of such *Lasterkataloge* from Hellenistic and Hellenistic-Jewish literature see Hans Lietzmann on Rom. i. 29–31, in *Handbuch zum neuen Testament*, Band III. *Die Briefe des Apostels Paulus.*

[2] A private interview between Jesus and his disciples is a favourite device of Mark's to introduce an explanatory comment. Cf. iv. 10, ix. 28, xiii. 3 sqq. (a comment on the hard saying which forecast the destruction of the temple).

[3] The first part of the saying is cited in Paul's discussion of the question of clean and unclean foods in Rom. xiv, and he adopts the same interpretation as Mark: πέπεισμαι ἐν Κυρίῳ ᾽Ιησοῦ ὅτι οὐδὲν κοινὸν δι᾽ ἑαυτοῦ (xiv. 14). I am now disposed to think that the expression ἐν Κυρίῳ Ιησοῦ (as distinct from the more usual ἐν Χριστῷ) indicates here (as in I Cor. ix. 1, xi. 33, I Thess. ii. 15) a reference to the historical Person and his teaching as transmitted in the tradition of the Church.

c

no doubt about the precise practices forbidden to Christians. Mark has observed, acutely enough, that this description of the vices of paganism might afford effective concrete illustration of what the Lord meant by 'things that proceed out of the heart and defile the man', and he has incorporated it into the record of the Sayings. The passage, Mark vii. 14–23, is therefore composite. The nucleus of it, the παραβολή of 15, was certainly handed down in the tradition of the sayings of the Lord; but the exegetical comment is composed of material developed within the *catechesis*, and by associating it with the saying Mark has facilitated the use of the saying itself for direct moral instruction.

It seems possible that some similar proceeding might give a clue to a passage which is a notorious *crux interpretum*, Mk. ix. 50: ἔχετε ἐν ἑαυτοῖς ἅλα καὶ εἰρηνεύετε ἐν ἀλλήλοις. The whole little paragraph, 49–50, is clearly composite. The nucleus, the *Bildwort* about savourless salt, certainly belongs to the central tradition of Sayings of the Lord. It occurs in all three Synoptic Gospels, and there is in the epistles no reference to salt[1] such as would suggest that it had any place in the catechetical scheme. The clause εἰρηνεύετε ἐν ἀλλήλοις, however, does seem to belong to that scheme. In I Thess. v. 12–22 we have a passage which fairly represents the section (E in the analysis above, p. 13) dealing with church order, and this includes the maxim, εἰρηνεύετε ἐν ἑαυτοῖς (v. 13). Similarly in Rom. xii. 18, which comes in a general exposition of Christian virtues (section C), we have εἰ δύνατον, τὸ ἐξ ὑμῶν, μετὰ πάντων ἀνθρώπων εἰρηνεύοντες, and in Rom. xiv. 19 the maxim is given application to a specific problem of church relations (that of divergent convictions about food and the observance of sacred days): τὰ τῆς εἰρήνης διώκωμεν καὶ τὰ τῆς οἰκοδομῆς τῆς εἰς ἀλλήλους. Again, among the final exhortations of II Corinthians we find τὸ αὐτὸ φρονεῖτε, εἰρηνεύετε (xiii. 11). And finally in Heb. xii. 14, in a context where the author is concerned with possible deviations from

---

[1] Ἅλατι ἠρτυμένος, in Col. iv. 6, even though both verb and substantive are also in Mk. ix. 50, does not appear to have any relevance to the saying.

Christian standards within the Church, we read, εἰρήνην διώκετε μετὰ πάντων. The general similarity of expression, and no less the common application (in all passages except Rom. xii. 18) to the theme of order within the Church, make it fairly certain that we are here dealing with a constant element in the τύπος διδαχῆς. Now while all three Synoptists reproduce the *Bildwort* about salt, they do not appear to know of any agreed interpretation or application of it. Luke (xiv. 34–5) offers no interpretation, but the context in which it stands suggests that he thought it had something to do with the unlimited self-abnegation required of the follower of Christ. For Matthew (v. 14) the disciples are themselves the 'salt' which will become useless if it loses its savour. Mark has taken it to refer in some way to the necessity of preserving peace in the church and so avoiding disorders—possibly having in mind the widespread idea that by taking a man's salt you have formed an indissoluble bond with him. At any rate we seem to have here one more instance in which the resources of the catechetical tradition have been drawn upon to supplement the tradition of Sayings of the Lord.

A similar instance is afforded by Matt. v. 16: οὕτως λαμψάτω τὸ φῶς ὑμῶν ἔμπροσθεν τῶν ἀνθρώπων ὅπως ἴδωσιν ὑμῶν τὰ καλὰ ἔργα καὶ δοξάσωσιν τὸν πατέρα ὑμῶν τὸν ἐν τοῖς οὐρανοῖς. This is offered as an application of the *Bildwort* about the lamp under the *modius* which, like the saying about salt, occurs in all three Synoptic Gospels, but without any agreed interpretation. Mark (iv. 21) has given it a context which makes it illustrate the certainty of the ultimate manifestation of 'the mystery of the Kingdom of God', at present veiled from οἱ ἔξω (cf. iv. 11 with 22). Luke reproduces it in the Marcan context, but also (xi. 33) in a quite different context, which suggests that it has something to do with the self-evidencing virtue of truth to the seeing eye (cf. the following saying, xi. 34–5). Matthew has made it quite clear that for him the lamp which is not to be hidden stands for the followers of Christ themselves (v. 14), and hence follows the application of the parable in v. 16. It must be confessed that the injunction, λαμψάτω τὸ φῶς ὑμῶν ἔμπροσθεν τῶν ἀνθρώπων ὅπως ἴδωσιν ὑμῶν τὰ καλὰ ἔργα is somewhat surprising when confronted

with such sayings as Matt. vi. 1: προσέχετε τὴν δικαιοσύνην
ὑμῶν μὴ ποιεῖν ἔμπροσθεν τῶν ἀνθρώπων πρὸς τὸ θεαθῆναι
αὐτοῖς, which at first sight seems to say precisely the opposite,
even echoing the language of v. 16 in a negative sense. But the
sentiment, that Christians should commend their faith to the
world by behaviour which outsiders can admire and respect,
is one which recurs in various forms of expression in the
epistles. Paul has it in the simplest terms, borrowed from the
Old Testament (Prov. iii. 4), in Rom. xii. 17: προνοούμενοι
καλὰ ἐνώπιον πάντων ἀνθρώπων. In I Peter iii. 16 it is enunciated
in terms which more distinctly betray the social context in
which it became urgently relevant: συνείδησιν ἔχοντες ἀγαθὴν,
ἵνα ἐν ᾧ καταλαλεῖσθε καταισχυνθῶσιν οἱ ἐπηρεάζοντες ὑμῶν
τὴν ἀγαθὴν ἐν Χριστῷ ἀναστροφήν. But the closest parallel
to Matt. v. 16 is in I Peter ii. 12, at the beginning of a long
section of the epistle (ii. 11–iii. 12) manifestly based upon the
catechetical pattern (though including some important themes
extraneous to the pattern): τὴν ἀναστροφὴν ὑμῶν ἐν τοῖς
ἔθνεσιν ἔχοντες καλήν, ἵνα ... ἐκ τῶν καλῶν ἔργων ἐποπτ-
εύοντες δοξάσωσιν τὸν θεόν. In this way, the writer adds,
they will be able to 'muzzle' the ignorance of silly people
(φιμοῦν τὴν τῶν ἀφρόνων ἀνθρώπων ἀγνωσίαν, ii. 15). The
inference seems plain: Matthew, having taken the *Bildwort* from
the common tradition of the Sayings of the Lord, without any
clear clue to its meaning or intention, has supplied an interpretation and application out of the catechetical tradition.

The examples here discussed do not afford a sufficiently wide
basis for induction to justify a firm conclusion, but the evidence,
so far as it goes, points towards some such view as the following. The 'Primitive Christian Catechism' (to adopt Archbishop Carrington's term), itself largely based on pre-Christian
models, provided a frame within which Christian teaching on
a wide range of topics could conveniently be organized for
paedagogic purposes. It appears that this framework was
utilized by some of those who made it their business to hand
down the Sayings of the Lord, as these appear in the gospels.
But it is clear that even where the evangelists seem to be
following the catechetical pattern as a general guide, they
were drawing from a channel of tradition quite independent

of the current τύπος διδαχῆς. It is probable, however, that material transmitted by any such channel was used to illustrate and enforce articles of the *catechesis*, and in this way such features as the image of the thief breaking in, and the insistence on prayer as essential to Christian preparedness for πειρασμός, were absorbed into the catechetical scheme, losing in the process something of their sharp outlines. In turn, a parable or dominical saying might receive a twist, or be given an application, to fit a 'moral' derived from the *catechesis*. This would explain how some parables in the gospels have suffered a certain shift of meaning.[1] The influence thus exerted upon the gospels by the *catechesis* calls for examination, but it was not, to all appearance, very far-reaching.

[1] See C. H. Dodd, *Parables of the Kingdom* (Nisbet, 1961), pp. 102-21, Jeremias, *Die Gleichnisse Jesu* (1962), pp. 45-64.

3 A Hidden Parable in the Fourth Gospel

It is commonly said that the Fourth Gospel contains no parables, such as are known to us from the Synoptic Gospels, but only allegories.[1] The Synoptic parable presents, whether in extended narrative or in brief similitude, a picture drawn from real life, which the hearers or readers will recognize as such, without the need for any 'decoding' of the elements of the picture. This is distinguishable from the artificial structure of symbols—needing to be interpreted in detail before the whole becomes fully intelligible—to which the term 'allegory' is often applied.[2] In the main it is true that the use of imagery in the Fourth Gospel conforms rather to the 'allegorical' style than to the 'parabolic'. Yet closer inspection reveals the fact that here and there, embedded in the Johannine discourses, true parables are to be found, though their character is partly concealed by the way in which they are absorbed into the flow of the argument. Thus Bultmann recognizes true parables (or *Bildworte*—the *Bildwort* being nothing but a condensed parable) in Jn. iii. 29a, the parable of Bridegroom and Bridegroom's Friend (as we might call it),[3] in viii. 35, the parable of Slave and Son,[4] and in xii. 35 the parable of the Benighted Traveller.[5] In each of these instances the imagery of the parable is at once exploited in allegorical fashion, yet this should not lead us to

[1] I have said something of the kind myself (*The Interpretation of the Fourth Gospel*, pp. 134-6), but I spoke in too absolute terms.

[2] See C. H. Dodd, *Parables of the Kingdom*, ch. I.

[3] 'Ein echtes Bildwort liegt vor, keine Allegorie' (*Das Johannesevangelium, ad loc.*).

[4] 'Scheint ursprünglich ein Bildwort gewesen zu sein', *op. cit., ad loc.*).

[5] 'Es scheint ein reines Bildwort zu sein, innerhalb dessen τὸ φῶς und σκότος ihren eigentlichen Sinn haben: das Tageslight und nächtliches Dunkel' (*op. cit., ad loc.*).

overlook the fact that the core of each passage is a realistic picture of a concrete human situation in this world. Similarly, in Jn. x. 1–5 the Bishop of Woolwich (Dr. J. A. T. Robinson) has acutely argued that we have, fused together and partly confused in the process, two parables entirely of Synoptic type. Down to the end of verse 5 there is nothing which is not a natural feature of pastoral life in Palestine. From verse 6 the imagery of the parable is exploited in elaborate allegorical fashion.[1] Further inspection will reveal other examples. The purpose of this essay is to point out an example which, I think, has been generally overlooked.

Jn. v. 19–30 is one of the most important christological passages in the Fourth Gospel, containing a careful definition of the relation of the Son to the Father, and of the functions of the Son as Saviour and Judge, which is regulative for the whole theology of the gospel.[2] Down to verse 20a, however, there is nothing which is *necessarily* christological.

Οὐ δύναται ὁ υἱὸς ποιεῖν ἀφ᾽ ἑαυτοῦ οὐδέν, ἂν μή τι βλέπῃ τὸν πατέρα ποιοῦντα· ἃ γὰρ ἂν ἐκεῖνος ποιῇ, ταῦτα καὶ ὁ υἱὸς ὁμοίως ποιεῖ. ὁ γὰρ πατὴρ φιλεῖ τὸν υἱὸν καὶ πάντα δείκνυσιν αὐτῷ ἃ αὐτὸς ποιεῖ.

On the face of it, we have a simple picture of a son apprenticed to his father's trade. The article with πατήρ and υἱός is generic, indicating that the statement applies to *any* father and *any* son. (This is normal in parables or *Bildworte*).[3] The son watches his father at work and imitates him; the father shows the son all the several operations of his craft, so that, by closely following the father's example, rather than experimenting at his own sweet will (ἀφ᾽ ἑαυτοῦ) he may himself become a master of the craft. After this point the elements of the picture are allegorized, the father and son of the parable becoming God the Father and

---

[1] J. A. T. Robinson, *Twelve New Testament Studies* (S.C.M. 1962), pp. 67–75.

[2] See *Interpretation*, pp. 320–328.

[3] So Bultmann *op. cit ad* xii, 45. Cf. ὁ ἰσχυρός (Mk. iii. 27), ὁ λύχνος (iv. 21), τὸ ἀκάθαρτον πνεῦμα (Mt. xii. 43), ὁ κώνωψ, ἡ κάμηλος (xxiii. 24) etc.

Christ the Son. The work of the Father is κρίνειν and ζωοποιεῖν, and the Son exercises these functions in dependence on Him. But the allegorical interpretation is in no way necessary to the understanding of the picture drawn in the parable, verses 19–20a.

The background of this picture is to be sought in a society in which crafts are hereditary, the techniques being handed down from father to son. This appears to have been normal in the skilled artisan class throughout the ancient Near and Middle East. A few concrete examples may serve to bring the background to life.

A papyrus from Oxyrhynchus,[1] dated about A.D. 25–26, and containing extracts from official documents of the reigns of Augustus and Tiberius, introduces us to a family of weavers (γέρδιοι) at that town. Tryphon son of Didymus (evidently a weaver himself) had three sons who followed the trade, Didymus, Dionysius, and Thoonis. Dionysius's son Trypho, born A.D. 8, also became a weaver; we have his receipts for payment of the weaver's tax (γερδιακόν) for the years 22–25 and 45–50. The younger Trypho, who was twice married, had (at least) two sons, Apion and Thoonis. The elder, Apion, is on record as paying γερδιακόν in 56. The younger son, Thoonis, was born in 52 or a little later. In 66 Tryphon apprenticed him to another weaver, Ptolemaeus, son of Pausirion. There would appear to be a special reason why in this instance the father did not himself initiate the son into the craft. In 52 Tryphon had secured exemption from military service on the ground that his eyesight was impaired by cararact (ὑποκεχυμένος ὀλίγον βλέπων); by 66 it was no doubt much worse. For the rest, we may fairly conclude that the technique of the craft passed down from Tryphon son of Didymus to Dionysius, from him to the younger Tryphon, and from him to Apion. And the best way for a boy to learn the art of weaving would be to watch his father at the loom: ἃ γὰρ ἂν ἐκεῖνος ποιῇ καὶ ὁ υἱὸς ὁμοίως ποιεῖ.

When the boy is apprenticed, his master stands *in loco*

---

[1] The facts here summarized are drawn from *Oxyrhynchus Papyri* nos. 285, 308, 282, 267, 37–8, 310, 39, 275 (in that order).

parentis. Apprenticeship was in fact analogous to adoption: the verb ἐκδιδόσθαι is used of both.[1] Thoonis's indenture certifies that Tryphon has given over (ἐκδιδόναι) his son to Ptolemy for the space of one year, to serve him and carry out all his instructions in respect of the art of weaving, as he himself knows it (διακονοῦντα καὶ ποιοῦντα πάντα τὰ ἐπιτασσόμενα αὐτῷ ὑπὸ τοῦ Πτολεμαίου κατὰ τὴν γερδιακὴν τέχνην, ὡς καὶ αὐτὸς ἐπίσταται). Similar language is used in a later indenture of A.D. 183,[2] by which Ischyrion son of Heradion of Oxyrhynchus apprentices his ward Thonis to the weaver Heraclas for five years. The boy is bound to carry out all instructions given him by the said teacher as in the case of other pupils in the like condition (ποιεῖν πάντα τὰ ἐπιταχθησόμενα αὐτῷ ὑπὸ τοῦ αὐτοῦ διδασκάλου ὡς ἐπὶ τῶν ὁμοίων μαθητῶν), and Heraclas agrees to teach the boy thoroughly the said art as he himself knows it (ἐκδιδάσκειν τὸν μαθητὴν τὴν δηλουμένην τέχνην ... καθὼς καὶ αὐτὸς ἐπίσταται). The last clause, evidently a standing feature of such indentures, may be compared with the phrase in the gospel, πάντα δείκνυσιν αὐτῷ ἃ αὐτὸς ποιεῖ. The father (it is assumed) will naturally do this; the master, *in loco parentis*, contracts to do so. To take one more example, in 155 Pamechotis apprenticed his slave-boy Chaeremon to Apollonius the shorthand-writer (σημειογράφος) for two years, 'to learn the shorthand signs which your son Dionysius knows' (πρὸς μάθησιν σημείων ὧν ἐπίσταται ὁ υἱός σου Διονύσιος).[3] It is assumed that the shorthand-writer has imparted his skill to his son, and he must do the same for the apprentice. The fee due to the teacher is to be paid in instalments, and the last instalment is not payable until the boy can write fluently and read without a mistake (τοῦ παιδὸς ἐκ παντὸς λόγου πέζου γράφοντος καὶ ἀναγινώσκοντος ἀμέμπτως)[4]

---

[1] E.g. O.P. 1206. ὁμολογοῦμεν ἡμεῖς ... ἐκδεδωκέναι σοι ʿΩρίωνι τὸν ἐξ ἡμῶν υἱὸν Πατερμοῦθιν ὡς ἐτῶν δύο εἰς υἱοθεσίαν.

[2] O.P. 724.   [3] O.P. 725.

[4] At the end of his apprenticeship the boy should be κατηρτισμένος ὡς ὁ διδάσκαλος, in the language of Lk. vi. 40, where the terms διδάσκαλος, μαθητής, are to be understood in the widest sense, of master and apprentice (as in the papyrus), as well as of a religious

The idea that the pupil stands in a kind of filial relation to his instructor reappears in a more sophisticated context in the language of some of the esoteric sects, religious or philosophical, which pullulated in the Hellenistic world. In the dialogues of the Hermetic Corpus, for example, it is common form for the sage who is imparting the revelation to be addressed as πάτερ, while he addresses the pupil as τέκνον or παῖ. The 'son' is sometimes identified as Tat, the legendary son of Hermes Trismegistos, and in most dialogues the 'father' is probably Hermes himself, but the dialogues are to be understood as reflecting the manner in which the doctrines of the school were transmitted, by oral instruction, from a 'father-in-God' (as we might say) to his 'son in the faith'.

The Hermetists were not unique in employing language of this kind, and along one line at least it seems possible to trace a connection between this notion of a kind of spiritual adoption and the simple practice of keeping a skilled craft in the family by transmission from father to son.[1] The hereditary principle seems to have been especially honoured among the metal-workers of ancient Egypt, who had the secret, not indeed of turning lead into gold, as their successors the alchemists claimed, but of altering the appearance of metals by means of a thin coating of gold or silver, of producing alloys which simulated the precious metals, and of applying enamels which imitated gold, silver, or precious stones. The earliest alchemical treatises are no more than simple recipes for carrying out such operations. These recipes, it seems, were handed down confidentially from father to son.[2] Out of this craft of metal-

---

teacher and his disciple. Lk. vi. 40, in fact, is a *Bildwort*, with the same background as Jn. v. 19, and conveying a similar idea.

[1] In what follows I summarize the account of the origins of alchemy given by A. J. Festugière in *La Revelation d'Hermés Trismegiste*, vol. I, particularly pp. 220–30.

[2] 'Il est croyable que, selon l'usage habituel en Orient, ces recettes se transmettaient de père en fils' (Festugière, *op. cit.*, p. 221). It is an inference, but a fairly certain inference. The argument might be formulated somewhat as follows: We know that in Egypt, as elsewhere, crafts tended to run in families. It is therefore *a priori* pro-

lurgical chemistry (if one may call it so) alchemy emerged, first
as a (pseudo-) philosophy and then as a kind of mystical
religion, and what had begun as a body of profitable trade
secrets to be kept in the family developed into a solemn deposit
of sacred doctrine not to be divulged to the profane. The
motive of secrecy was essential to the cult.[1] It was related that
Ostanes, the legendary founder, had taken steps, in prospect
of death, to ensure that his mystery should be known to no one
but his son; and the implication is that the example should be
followed by his successors. Here we have at least one con-
tributory factor in the establishment of the convention which
was common to most if not all of the occult sciences, and which
we have observed in the philosophical *Hermetica*.

There is perhaps something analogous to this in the Hebrew
order of prophets. The disciples of a נָבִיא are called his
'sons',[2] and they address him as אָבִי.[3] Collectively the members
of the prophetic order are בְּנֵי הַנְּבִיאִים.[4] If you meet a stray
company of נְבִיאִים, it is natural to ask, 'Who is their father?'[5]
But a more pertinent parallel, perhaps, is to be found in the
Jewish Wisdom Literature, where the address, 'My son', is
common form,[6] just as it is in the *Hermetica*. Here the possible
influence of the Hellenistic convention is not to be excluded,

---

bable that this would be the case in so highly esteemed a craft as
that of metal-working. We know also that the alchemists borrowed
the recipes from the craftsmen who were their predecessors. It is
therefore extremely probable that they similarly borrowed the
tradition by which the recipes passed from father to son.

[1] So Festugière, *op. cit.*, p. 230: 'La defense de divulguer la revelation, ou de moins de la transmettre à d'autres qu'à son propre fils,
e'est là un thème constant dans les sciences occultes. Nous le
retrouvons à chaque page.'

[2] I Kings xiii. 11–13; cf. Amos vii. 14.   [3] II Kings ii. 12.

[4] II Kings ii. 3–7, etc.   [5] I Sam. x. 12.

[6] Prov. i. 8, ii. 1, iii. 1 *et passim*. Sir. ii. 2 *et passim*. Note especially Prov. iv. 11, שִׁמְעוּ בָנִים מוּסַר אָב Sir. iii. 2, ἐμοῦ τοῦ πατρὸς
ἀκούσατε τέκνα. Exceptionally, the instruction may be attributed
to a 'mother', Prov. xxxi. 1.

but a more direct antecedent, no doubt, is the established principle of Judaism that the father of a family was under obligation to teach his son;[1] to teach him, primarily, the Torah and the ancestral traditions;[2] but the teaching included also reading and writing and the elements of a general education.

There can be little doubt that it included also, where this was appropriate, the teaching of the family trade or craft, though direct and specific evidence for this seems hard to come by. That hereditary crafts were known among the Jews as elsewhere we might fairly assume, and indeed it seems to be implied in the use of language. The name for a trade guild is מִשְׁפָּחָה[3] literally a 'family' or 'clan'. Its members are called 'sons',[4] its head, 'father'.[5] Similarly the legendary founder of an art or craft is the 'father' of its practitioners.[6] In II Chron. ii. 12. אָבִי appears to denote professional status. The king of Tyre sends to Solomon a highly skilled craftsman (אִישׁ־חָכָם יוֹדֵעַ בִּינָה) for work on the temple, providing him with a flattering testimonial. He names him 'Father Huram' (חוּרָם אָב), meaning, apparently, that he is a master of the craft,

---

[1] See G. F. Moore, *Judaism*, vol. II, pp. 127 sqq. R. de Vaux, *Les Institutions de l' Ancien Testament*, vol. I, pp. 120 sqq. L. Dürr, *Das Erziehungswesen im Alten Testament und im antiken Orient*, in *Mitteilungen der vorderasiatischen-ägyptischen Gesellschaft*, vol. 36, no. 2, part 3 section 2, pp. 106 sqq. For references to Jewish sources I am greatly indebted to the Rev. E. W. Heaton, author of *Everyday Life in Old Testament Times*.

[2] 8 Exod. xii. 26–7; Deut. iv. 9–10, vi. 7, 20 sqq., xxxii. 7, 46, etc.

[3] E.g. I Chron. iv. 21: מִשְׁפְּחוֹת בֵּית עֲבֹדַת הַבֻּץ 'the guilds of linen workers'.

[4] Nehem. iii. 8: בֶּן־הָרַקָּחִים, 'a member of the guild of perfumiers', 31, בֶּן־הַצֹּרְפִי, 'a member of the goldsmiths' guild'.

[5] So perhaps I Chron. iv. 14, אֲבִי גֵּיא חֲרָשִׁים.

[6] Genesis iv. 31: Jubal was 'the father of all such as handle the harp or pipe,' i.e. the founder of the art; the Targum renders אב by רבהון, 'their teacher'. It is however quite possible that these forms of instrumental music were originally the prerogative of certain families (in the literal sense), like the McCrimmons and other families of hereditary pipers in Scotland.

and no mere journeyman—perhaps even suggesting that he stands 'at the head of the profession'.[1] As it happens, we are informed of two Jewish families in which a highly specialized trade was hereditary: one of them baked the shewbread, the other manufactured incense for the temple.[2] In the New Testament we have two instances, one certain, the other probable, of hereditary crafts. James and John, the sons of Zebedee, followed their father's trade of fishing (Mk. i. 19–20), and Jesus himself, according to Mk. vi. 3, was a τέκτων, and, according to Matt. xiii. 55, the son of a τέκτων.[3] In all such cases it is natural to suppose that the father taught his sons. It was indeed laid down by the Rabbis that a father was obliged to teach his son a trade or handicraft. Rabbi Judah (ben Ilai) said, 'A man who does not teach his son a trade or handicraft teaches him robbery'.[4] Yet it is not clear that such expressions are to be taken *au pied de la lettre*. We read, for example, that 'R. Meir said, "A man should always teach his son a cleanly craft". R. Gorion of Zaida said in the name of R. Guria: "A man

---

[1] This paragon of craftsmen could certainly not be accused of undue specialization. According to his royal patron, he was 'skilful to work in gold, and in silver, in brass, in iron, in stone and in timber, in purple, in blue and in fine linen, and in crimson; also to grave any manner of graving, and to devise any device'! Yet the combination of metals with textiles is perhaps not so surprising as it appears at first sight. Metallurgical techniques occur along with dyeing in the recipes of the alchemists (Festugière, *op. cit.*, pp. 221–2).

[2] *Yoma* 3. 11. The 'house of Garmu' baked the shewbread, the 'house of Abtinas' prepared the incense. The context shows that the monopoly aroused some resentment.

[3] Dürr, *op. cit.*, p. 108, takes the two expressions to be synonymous, 'son of a carpenter' meaning no more than one who practices the trade of carpentry. But Matthew's expression is ὁ τοῦ τέκτονος υἱός, and the two articles seem to rule out Dürr's interpretation. Besides, the context, in Matthew as in Mark, requires a reference to family relationship.

[4] *Pal. Kiddushin*, 61a, cited by Moore, *op. cit.*, p. 127, Strack-Billerbeck, *Kommentar zum N.T.*, vol. II, p. 745.

should not teach his son to be an ass-driver or a camel-driver or a sailor or a herdman or a shop-keeper, for their craft is the craft of robbers".[1] Again, 'R. Kappara said, "a man should always teach his son a clean and light trade." Which is such? R. Hisda said, "Needle stitching." '[2] It seems clear that such sayings do not contemplate strictly hereditary trades, since it is presupposed that the father can *choose* his son's vocation. The expression, ‏ילמד אדם את בנו אמנות‎ must be understood in the sense that a man should *have his son taught*[3]—by binding him apprentice, no doubt. Nevertheless the form of expression preserves the idea that the father is in principle the teacher of his son, and clearly where the trade did actually run in the family this norm would be followed.

In spite, therefore, of the comparative paucity of direct evidence, it seems clear that among the Jews of Palestine, as in the Hellenistic world, it was normal for an artisan father to teach the technique of his trade to his son.[4] We have thus discovered a society such as was postulated at the beginning (p. 32) for the background of the passage we are considering. When the evangelist speaks of a father who, because he loves his son, shows him everything that he himself does,[5] and of a son who, instead of acting on his own initiative, watches his

---

[1] *Kiddushin* 4. 14 in *Mishna* (ed. Danby), p. 329.

[2] *Berachoth* 63a (ed. Cohen).

[3] Strack-Billerbeck render, correctly, 'erlernen lassen'.

[4] De Vaux speaks categorically: 'On travaillait sous le régime de l'atelier familiale, où le père transmittait le métier a son fils' (*op. cit.*, p. 120). Similarly Moore, *loc. cit.* Dürr is somewhat more guarded: 'Als Regel ist wohl auch hier anzunehmen dass der Sohn das Handwerk des Vaters lernte, dieses also in der Familie erblich war' (*op. cit.*, 108). I should state the case somewhat differently: it is a sufficiently secure inference from the evidence that hereditary crafts existed among the Jews, and, that being so, it may further be inferred that in such crafts the father was normally the teacher; for which also there is *some*, though not copious, direct evidence.

[5] Ὁ πατὴρ φιλεῖ τὸν υἱὸν αὐτοῦ καὶ πάντα δείκνυσιν αὐτῷ ἃ αὐτὸς ποιεῖ. C. Sir. xxx. 1–3: Ὁ ἀγαπῶν τὸν υἱὸν αὐτοῦ ... ὁ παιδεύων τὸν υἱὸν αὐτοῦ ... ὁ διδάσκων τὸν υἱὸν αὐτοῦ.

father at work and does exactly as he does, he is describing in the simplest and most realistic terms a perfectly familiar situation in everyday life. It is a significant detail that the apprentice *watches* his father at work. The picture is drawn from artisan life; the father is one who works with his hands, and the son learns by copying his actions. This detail is not made use of in the theological exposition which follows;[1] it is not a feature dictated by the requirements of the deeper meaning which is to be conveyed. It is integral to the scene as realistically conceived. It is precisely at this point that the difference between the parable and the allegory reveals itself most clearly. Our passage conforms to all criteria for the true parable. It might be called, the parable of the Son as Apprentice.

By the nature of its contents, then, this passage readily falls into the class of parables known to us from the Synoptic Gospels. Further, its *form* has Synoptic analogues. Its basic structure is simple: two general categorical clauses forming an antithesis, followed by an explanatory clause.

A. (Negation) A son learning his trade can do nothing but what he sees his father doing.
B. (Affirmation) What he sees his father doing, the son does likewise.
C. (Explanation) For the father shows him all that he is doing.

We find a similar pattern in Lk. viii. 16 (and with verbal differences in Matt. v. 15):

A. (Negation) No one lights a lamp and hides it under a *modius*.
B. (Affirmation) He puts it on the lampstand.
C. (Explanation) So that it may give light to all who enter.

Lk. vi. 40, already cited (p. 33) because the situation it depicts

---

[1] Undoubtedly, when once the allegorical approach is established in the reader's mind he will discover symbolic meanings in all manner of details; and so here the words βλέπῃ τὸν πατέρα will remind him of the highly theological doctrine of vi. 46, ὁ ὢν παρὰ τοῦ θεοῦ οὗτος ἑώρακεν τὸν πατέρα, and this was probably intended by the evangelist; but it is not the theology that has produced the realistic detail of the parable.

is similar to that of our passage, might be regarded as an incomplete example of the same pattern, the supplementary third clause being here unnecessary.

A. A pupil cannot be superior to his teacher.
B. His training finished, he may become like his teacher.

Lk. xii. 47–8 has a fundamentally similar structure.

A. A slave who disobeys knowingly will be severely beaten.
B. A slave who disobeys in ignorance will be let off lightly.

The sentence which follows in 48b has the effect of the usual explanatory clause: to whom much is given, from him much will be expected. Finally Lk. xi. 21–2, though more complex in structure, is basically similar.

A. When a strong man stands guard in arms his property is safe.
B. When a stronger arrives, he is stripped of his arms and his goods are plundered.

No supplementary clause is called for, because the ὅταν, ἐπάν, clauses sufficiently indicate the conditions which determine the outcome, favourable or unfavourable.

There is thus good ground for believing that the parable of the Son as Apprentice was not originally composed by the author of the Fourth Gospel, but drawn by him from the general reservoir of primary tradition which also supplied parables to the other evangelists. Can we go further? If it is true that Jesus was himself both τέκτων and τέκτονος υἱός, then it is hardly too bold a conjecture that we may have here an echo of his own words, recalling memories of the years of his youth when he learnt his trade in the family workshop at Nazareth.

4 Behind a Johannine Dialogue

Among the various 'forms' in which the Church's witness to the teaching and the saving work of Christ is presented in the gospels, the one most characteristic of the Fourth Gospel is the elaborately wrought dramatic dialogue. The Johannine dialogue is an original literary creation, having in some respects more affinity with Hellenistic models than with the dialogues of the Synoptic Gospels or their rabbinic analogues.[1] The present study is directed towards a problem which may be stated thus: granted that the literary form of these dialogues is the original work of the Fourth Evangelist, how far do their character and contents point to any known situation in the early Church as providing their background, or '*Sitz im Leben*', and how are they related to the contents of other parts of the gospel tradition. This has a bearing upon the wider problem of the value of the Fourth Gospel as a source of historical information. I shall here take as a specimen one particular dialogue, and examine it from this point of view.

The long dialogue in John viii. 31–58, one of the most powerful and most carefully composed in the Fourth Gospel, forms a unit within the sequence of controversial dialogues staged at the Feast of Tabernacles (vii–viii).[2] It is held together by recurrent references to Abraham.[3] In the first part of the dialogue he appears as the ancestor of the Jewish people, in the latter part as a venerated figure of the past whose rôle in history, essentially transitory, is a foil to the eternal being of

[1] C. H. Dodd, 'The Dialogue Form in the Gospels', in *Bulletin of the John Rylands Library*, vol. xxxvii, no. 1 (Sept. 1954), partly reproduced in *Historical Tradition in the Fourth Gospel* (C.U.P., 1963).

[2] See C. H. Dodd, *The Interpretation of the Fourth Gospel*, pp. 345–54.

[3] His name, not found elsewhere in the Johannine writings, occurs 10 times in this context.

D

Christ. But there is a deeper unity of theme, for the proposition which is the pivot of the argument in the first part, ἐγὼ ἐκ τοῦ θεοῦ ἐξῆλθον καὶ ἥκω (42), and the final statement πρὶν Ἀβραὰμ γενέσθαι ἐγὼ εἰμί (58), are complementary. There is no sharp break between the two parts. The dialogue flows on, passing, after this evangelist's manner, into monologue,[1] and working up to the impressive conclusion in verse 58. A transition, however, may be marked at verse 47, which states the conclusion upon the theme treated thus far, before the oracular saying of 51 launches the second theme.

It is with the first part, viii. 31–47, that we shall here be concerned. The debate is lively and dramatic, proceeding logically to a clear (and devastating) conclusion. But it presents one serious difficulty: as the passage stands, a group of Jews who have been described as 'believers' are accused of attempted murder, and roundly denounced as children of the devil. Most commentators have recognized the difficulty, and they have adopted various expedients for resolving it. As a record of an historical incident, the passage fails to convince; we feel that at least some essential step must have been left out. If, on the other hand, we regard it, with many commentators, as a reflection of controversies between the Church and the Synagogue round about A.D. 100, it is still not clear why the Synagogue should be represented by 'believing' Jews.

It will be well to start by examining more closely the actual terms in which the evangelist introduces the interlocutors in the dialogue: οἱ πεπιστευκότες αὐτῷ Ἰουδαῖοι. Unless we are prepared to have recourse to some theory of interpolation or disarrangement, it seems inevitable that this phrase should be taken as referring back to the preceding sentence: ταῦτα αὐτοῦ λαλοῦντος πολλοὶ ἐπίστευσαν εἰς αὐτόν. Indeed, the expression, οἱ πεπιστευκότες, is hardly perspicuous unless there has been some previous indication that such a class of persons existed. The only objection to understanding the two clauses as referring to the same persons is based upon the difference between πιστεύειν εἰς αὐτόν and πιστεύειν αὐτῷ. As a rule, in this gospel, the latter expression means giving credence to

---

[1] See *Interpretation*, p. 400.

what Jesus (or another, according to the context) has said, while the former connotes a personal relation to him.[1] Yet if we suppose that the phrase πολλοὶ ἐπίστευσαν εἰς αὐτόν speaks of those who gave their allegiance to Christ, and that οἱ πεπιστευκότες αὐτῷ signifies a group who had not gone so far as that, though they were ready to believe what he said, even so we are not rid of our difficulty, for these very persons who are here described as πεπιστευκότες αὐτῷ are in verse 46 reproached in the terms, διὰ τί ὑμεῖς οὐ πιστεύετέ μοι: It is probable that we should not here press the usual distinction between πιστεύειν εἰς αὐτόν and πιστεύειν αὐτῷ, but regard it as a mere stylistic variation. In that case the relation between the verb in verse 30 and the participle in verse 31 is normal. The verb in the aorist refers to a single, specific act: these persons, upon a day, made an act of faith. Quite properly, their consequent status is described in the perfect participle of the same verb, the perfect standing for the 'punctilinear' *Aktionsart*. These persons, then, became believers and remained such down to the moment to which the ensuing narrative refers. That is at any rate the natural, *prima facie*, meaning of the words.

This use of the perfect participle of πιστεύειν is found elsewhere. Thus in Acts xxi. 20 James, wishing to impress upon Paul the weight of opinion in the Church adverse to his mission, says, Θεωρεῖς, ἀδελφέ, πόσαι μυριάδες εἰσὶν ἐν τοῖς 'Ιουδαίοις τῶν πεπιστευκότων—'what myriads of converts there are among the Jews'—myriads, that is, of persons who became Christians and remain Christians. Similarly in Acts xv. 45 we have, τινὲς τῶν ἀπὸ τῆς αἱρέσεως τῶν φαρισαίων πεπιστευκότες. It would appear, then, that the meaning conveyed by the phrase, οἱ πεπιστευκότες 'Ιουδαῖοι, to readers in the Greek-speaking Church in the latter part of the first century, was 'Jewish converts to Christianity', or, as we say, 'Jewish Christians'. In Acts x. 45 the same meaning is conveyed by the phrase, οἱ ἐκ περιτομῆς πιστοί, the adjective being used in place of the participle. In the same sense we are probably to understand οἱ ἐκ περιτομῆς in Acts xi. 2, since Peter,

---

[1] See *Interpretation*, pp. 182–3, and cf. Bultmann, *Das Johannes-Evangelium*, p. 189 n. 1.

addressing them, speaks of Gentile converts in these terms: τὴν ἴσην δωρεὰν ἔδωκεν αὐτοῖς ὁ θεὸς ὡς καὶ ἡμῖν πιστεύσασιν ἐπὶ τὸν Κύριον Ἰησοῦν Χριστόν, where πιστεύσασιν, whatever its formal grammatical connection, must in sense refer both to αὐτοῖς and to ἡμῖν: *both* Jews *and* Gentiles performed the act of faith and consequently are Christians. The former are οἱ ἐκ περιτομῆς πιστοί, or οἱ πεπιστευκότες Ἰουδαῖοι.

'Jewish Christians', then; but we note that in most of these places they are not only Jewish by origin but also take what we may call a Jewish-national standpoint. James, speaking, perhaps with pardonable exaggeration, of the 'tens of thousands' of Jewish Christians, claims that they are *all* devoted to the Torah, and in consequence highly critical of Paul. Similarly, in Acts xi. 2 οἱ ἐκ περιτομῆς (scil. πιστοί) denounce Peter for his unlawful table-fellowship with uncircumcised Gentiles, and in Acts xv. 5 the Jewish Christians described as converted Pharisees offer opposition to the missionary policy of Paul and Barnabas, and insist that their Gentile converts shall be circumcised.

These two points, circumcision and table-fellowship, are crucial in Paul's polemic in the epistle to the Galatians. The persons who provoked the controversy are there called οἱ ἐκ περιτομῆς (Gal. ii. 12, cf. Acts xi. 2). The expression in itself could mean either 'Jews' simply, or 'those who advocate circumcision', but it is most probably to be understood as meaning Jewish Christians,[1] just as οἱ λοιποὶ Ἰουδαῖοι in Gal. ii. 13 are obviously *Christian* Jews. The group which intimidated Peter, called οἱ ἐκ περιτομῆς, is probably to be conceived as either coextensive, or as overlapping, with the emissaries of James (with his 'myriads' of πεπιστευκότες Ἰουδαῖοι).

It appears, then, that 'Jewish believers', οἱ πεπιστευκότες Ἰουδαῖοι, οἱ ἐν τοῖς Ἰουδαίοις πεπιστευκότες, οἱ ἐκ περιτομῆς πιστοί, were regarded, in circles from which the Acts and the Pauline epistles emanate, as a group not only Jewish by birth (which would have included Paul himself and several of his

---

[1] In Col. iv. 11 οἱ ὄντες ἐκ τῆς περιτομῆς are clearly *Christian* Jews, but in this place without any suggestion of 'Judaizing'.

collaborators), but also prejudiced by their conservative attachment to the Jewish national tradition. The tension between this group and the growing Gentile majority is reflected in the Pauline epistles (*c.* A.D. 50–65), in the Acts of the Apostles (perhaps twenty to thirty years later), and in the Pastoral Epistles (probably not far from A.D. 100), for in Tit. i. 10 various disturbers of discipline are denounced, μάλιστα οἱ ἐκ τῆς περιτομῆς.[1] At any time, therefore, between (say) A.D. 50 and 100 οἱ πεπιστευκότες Ἰουδαῖοι would be recognized as professed Christians of Jewish origin likely to be opposed to beliefs and practices now accepted by the Church at large.

It is therefore probable that to readers of the Fourth Gospel acquainted with the situation in the Church in their time the 'believing Jews' of viii. 30–1 would bring to mind Jewish converts within the Church, and they would read these verses as if the Lord were addressing such Jewish Christians in the words 'If you continue to follow my teaching, then you are in the true sense "disciples" '—μαθηταί being one of the standard terms for members of the Church in the Acts. We may fairly suppose that the evangelist himself intended the interlocutors in the dialogue to represent 'Judaizing' Christians rather than Jews outside the Church.[2] This does not, it is true, altogether overcome the difficulty raised by the unsparing condemnation of these 'believers'. But Paul, who felt the influence of the 'Judaizers' to be pernicious in the extreme, goes so far as to pronounce an anathema upon them (Gal. i. 6–9). They are in some sort Christians, for they preach a Gospel (though a 'different Gospel'), indeed they preach Christ

[1] These must be *Christian* Jews, since they are properly amenable to the discipline of the Church (it is Titus's duty to 'bridle' them), though they rebel against it. Some of their tenets may be inferred from I Tim. i. 6–11, Tit. i. 14–15 iii. 9, etc.

[2] The suggestion is of course not new. Loisy, *Le Quatrième Évangile*, 1903, pp. 566 sqq., comments, 'On peut se demander si l'auteur n'a pas aussi' (*scil.* as well as Jews as such) 'en vue des chrétiens absolument judaïsants, ou retombés dans le judaïsme'. But this note does not reappear in the second edition, 1921.

(though 'another Christ'). Yet they are 'anathema', i.e. outside
the sphere of salvation. Those whom they succeed in persuad-
ing to undergo circumcision (the rite by which the individual
appropriates the benefits of the covenant with Abraham) forfeit
all the benefits which Christ bestows (Χριστὸς ὑμᾶς οὐδὲν
ὠφελήσει, Gal. v. 2), for to claim the 'inheritance' (of Abraham)
on the ground of fulfilment of the Law's commands empties
faith of its content and nullifies the promise (κεκένωται ἡ
πίστις καὶ κατήργηται ἡ ἐπαγγελία, Rom. iv. 14). In Gal. ii.
15–16 it is implied that the 'Judaizers' held that those of Jewish
birth (φύσει Ἰουδαῖοι) did not *need* to be justified by faith.
Paul retorts that this means that 'Christ died for nothing' (ii.
21), and maintains that born Jews like Peter and himself, no
less than 'sinners of the Gentiles' had to seek justification by
faith in Christ (καὶ ἡμεῖς ἐπιστεύσαμεν ἵνα δικαιωθῶμεν).

The attitude adopted by the 'believing Jews' of John viii.
is similar to that which Paul condemns so roundly. Offered
'liberation'[1] by Christ, they retort that being children of
Abraham they do not *need* liberation. Paul would have taken
the view that in doing so they were putting themselves outside
the pale of Christianity and forfeiting its benefits. John, we
may suppose, takes the same view. They have been warned to
'dwell in the word' of Christ (ἐάν μείνητε ἐν τῷ λόγῳ τῷ ἐμῷ).
In his view they are clearly not doing so. The consequence of
not 'dwelling in the word' we may gather from II John 9,
πᾶς ὁ . . . μὴ μένων ἐν τῇ διδαχῇ τοῦ Χριστοῦ θεὸν οὐκ ἔχει ·ὁ
μένων ἐν τῇ διδαχῇ οὗτος καὶ τὸν πατέρα καὶ τὸν υἱὸν ἔχει. In
effect (though still claiming to be 'believers') the 'Judaistic'
Christians have emptied their faith of its content (κεκένωται
ἡ πίστις), and are where they were before they made the act
of faith recorded in verse 30. Hence in what follows they are
treated as if they were Jews *simpliciter*, and not believing Jews.
They are even identified with the Jews who sought to compass
the death of Christ. This, though somewhat startling to us,
would not have seemed so extravagant (e.g.) to the Author to

---

[1] We may recall that ἀπελευθέρωσις is a synonym for ἀπολύτρωσις.
It is 'redemption' (in Pauline terms) that they are offered, and reject
as unnecessary for children of Abraham.

the Hebrews, who warns Christians in danger of lapsing from the faith[1] that in doing so they would be 'crucifying the Son of God over again' (ἀνασταυροῦντας ἑαυτοῖς τὸν υἱὸν τοῦ θεοῦ) (Heb. vi. 6).

If therefore we enquire for the '*Sitz im Leben*', or historical situation within which this dialogue may have taken form, a reasonable hypothesis would be that it goes back to the struggle waged throughout the latter half of the first century[2] in defence of the supra-national character of the Church against those who sought to maintain within it the traditional privilege of the Jew.

We may test this hypothesis by examining the course taken by the debate. It turns upon three points mainly, which may be put briefly as follows: (i) liberty and servitude, (ii) descent from Abraham, (iii) sonship to God. These three points are cardinal also in Paul's polemic in Galatians.[3] In John viii, as in Galatians, there is a contrast between the son and the slave (Jn. viii. 35, Gal. iv. 3–7). In both the transition from the concept 'son of Abraham' to the concept 'son of God' is made tacitly, as if it might be taken for granted (Jn. viii. 39–41, Gal. iii. 26, 29). In the course of the controversy John and Paul alike blur the distinction between Christian and non-Christian Jews, since the position taken by the 'Judaizing' Christians is, in the judgment of both writers, indistinguishable from that of non-Christian Jews, so far as the points at issue are concerned. We can well believe that we are overhearing different phases of the same controversy.

The difference of treatment, however, is not less marked

[1] Into 'liberal Judaism', like that of Philo, as I believe, rather than into 'Gnosticism' or semi-paganism.

[2] It may well have gone on still longer, but it is possible that the dialogue may have taken shape (as also other Johannine dialogues) perhaps over a period of years, before it was finally woven into the structure of the gospel, which itself, in view of recent evidence, cannot now be dated more than a very few years (if any) after A.D. 100.

[3] Liberty, Gal. iv. 1–10, v. 1, 14; descent from Abraham, iii. 7–18, iv. 21–31; sonship to God, iii. 26–7, iv. 4–7.

than the community of theme. It is to be noted in the first place that questions which are extremely prominent in Paul are not mentioned in John, notably those of circumcision and of the continuing obligation of the Mosaic Law. The sole question is whether Jewish Christians are or are not loyal to the teaching of Christ (ἐὰν μείνητε ἐν τῷ λόγῳ τῷ ἐμῷ). It may be that by the time, or in the circle, in which John wrote, these questions were no longer alive, or it may be that he considered them merely consequential and not fundamental issues. In any case he does not here stand on Pauline ground.

As for the points which both writers discuss, it is common ground that Christ offers true liberty (though Paul has the rather Hebraic sounding τῇ ἐλευθερίᾳ ἠλευθέρωσεν[1] and John the very Greek sounding ὄντως ἐλεύθεροι). In both, the 'Judaizers' claim that such liberty is the inherent prerogative of descendants of Abraham.[2] But the ways in which the two deal with this claim are widely different. Paul argues that law in principle enslaves, and therefore there is no true liberty unless the obligations of the law are abrogated by the same authority that established them. John argues in different terms. He pre-supposes two established axioms of popular Hellenistic philosophy: (*a*) that wisdom, or knowledge of truth, alone makes a man free: γνώσεσθε τὴν ἀλήθειαν καὶ ἡ ἀλήθεια ἐλευθερώσει ὑμᾶς = μόνος ὁ σοφὸς ἐλεύθερος,[3] and (*b*) that the sinner is a slave: πᾶς

---

[1] So probably read Gal. v. 1, with ℵ B, etc. The presence of the article distinguishes it from the common use of the cognate dative as an equivalent of the Hebrew infinitive absolute in the LXX and the N.T., yet it has a ring of that idiom.

[2] So explicitly Jn. viii. 33, implicitly in Paul, for the allegorical interpretation of the scripture about Hagar and Sarah in Gal. iv. 21–31 is pretty clearly directed against an interpretation which guaranteed to the Jewish nation the 'inheritance' of Isaac.

[3] This is a Stoic commonplace. See passages cited in Wetstein and in Bauer, *ad loc.* Philo's tractate, Περὶ τοῦ πάντα σπουδαῖον ἐλεύθερον εἶναι, is pure Stoicism illustrated with occasional quotations from the O.T. That Christian 'liberty' is not the same thing as Stoic 'liberty' goes without saying.

ὁ ποιῶν τὴν ἁμαρτίαν δοῦλός ἐστιν[1] = οὐδεὶς ἁμαρτάνων ἐλεύθερός ἐστιν.[2] Upon these presuppositions, he argues, the Jews are not free, since (*a*) their incomprehension of the teaching of Christ shows them to be *incapable* of 'knowing the truth' (cf. 43, οὐ δύνασθε ἀκούειν τὸν λόγον τὸν ἐμόν), and (*b*) their moral obliquity proves them to be slaves (34 with 44). The argument is conducted in a context of thought remote from Paul's rabbinism.

Similarly, the argument rebutting the claim to privilege based on descent from Abraham is conducted on lines radically different from Paul's. For him, it is of the utmost importance to establish that Christians, and not Jews who reject the Gospel, are σπέρμα τοῦ Ἀβραάμ. This expression, he holds, as used in Scripture, means (*a*) Christ (Gal. iii. 16–17), and (*b*) those who, through a faith which reproduces the faith of Abraham, are incorporate in Christ (Rom. iv. 16–25, Gal. iii. 7–29).[3] The expression, σπέρμα του Ἀβραάμ, therefore, contains for him the very central significance of the Gospel. For John it has no such significance. He can readily grant that the Jews are σπέρμα Ἀβραάμ (37), in the sense in which any ordinary person would understand the term: they trace their pedigree from an historical person of that name. That, the evangelist admits, is a plain fact—but it is irrelevant. The question is, do the descendants of Abraham reproduce the character and behaviour of their ancestor—his 'works' (33), not his faith, as in Paul. The Jews

---

[1] So read Jn. viii. 34, with Db, Sinaitic Syriac, Clement of Alexandria. The addition of τῆς ἁμαρτίας may be due to a reminiscence of Pauline teaching, cf. Rom. vi. 6–18. It is not here called for by the context. Indeed, it makes the transition to verse 35 extremely awkward: it is not the slave *of sin* who fails to abide in the house for ever! John is concerned with the servile *status* as such. So indeed is Paul, where he is dealing directly with the 'Judaistic' problem in Galatians.

[2] Epictetus, *Diss.* II. i. 23. It is another Stoic commonplace; see again Wetstein *ad loc.* It is unnecessary to labour the point that what Epictetus means by ἁμαρτάνων and what John means by ποιῶν ἁμαρτίαν are different things.

[3] Where he is not talking theology Paul is prepared to use σπέρμα Ἀβραάμ in its natural sense, II Cor. xi. 23.

are challenged to show that they 'do the works of Abraham' (39).[1] This points to an approach to the idea of Abraham as a pattern to his descendants from a standpoint different from Paul's; cf. James ii. 21, Ἀβραὰμ ὁ πατὴρ ἡμῶν οὐκ ἐξ ἔργων ἐδικαιώθη; The intention is to insist that it is moral likeness to Abraham, and not physical descent from him, that has religious value; and this moral likeness is lacking in those who seek to compass the death of Christ.

Once again, the concept of sonship to God is not treated on Pauline lines. For Paul the Christian is a child of God by adoption (υἱοθεσία, Gal. iv. 5). Such adoption is dependent on incorporation into Christ by baptism on the basis of faith

---

[1] In the crucial verses, 38 and 39, neither text nor interpretation is certain. To start with 39, in the conditional sentence the majority of MSS. read ἦτε in the protasis and ἐποιεῖτε (or ἐποιεῖτε ἄν) in the apodosis, giving an 'unreal' conditional sentence of normal form: 'If you were Abraham's children (which you are not) you would do the works of Abraham (as you do not)'. B alone gives ἐστὲ in the protasis and ποιεῖτε in the apodosis, and this reading is supported by the Latin Vulgate, by Origen in the majority of his citations (though he wavers—or at least his MSS. do), and by Augustine. This also gives a perfectly regular form of conditional sentence, in which the verb in the apodosis may be either indicative or imperative. A number of MSS. have a mixed form, with ἐστὲ . . . ἐποιεῖτε(ἄν). This is of course entirely irregular, but it would probably have to be construed as an 'unreal' conditional sentence, as if ἦτε were read. If we take it as such, the meaning is that the Jews are not children of Abraham, since they do not 'do the works of Abraham'. But their claim to descent from Abraham has already been expressly conceded (οἶδα ὅτι σπέρμα Ἀβραάμ ἐστε), and an attempt to distinguish between σπέρμα (conceded) and τέκνα (denied) seems quite arbitrary. If the text of B is accepted, it seems best to take ποιεῖτε as imperative. 'If (as I have already granted) you are descendants of Abraham, then behave as such.' If so, then we should be disposed to take ποιεῖτε in 38 in the same way. In that case, the 'father' of the Jews is Abraham. If on the other hand ποιεῖτε is taken as indicative, the 'father' is someone other than Abraham— the devil, as it turns out. But this anticipation of the conclusion of

(Gal. iii. 27–8). It is verified by the utterance of the Spirit within, Ἀββᾶ ὁ πατήρ (Gal. iv. 6, the ὅτι being declaratory, not causal). John, in this passage, predicates sonship to God only of Christ, denying it of the Jews who falsely claim it. From other passages we learn that it is those who receive the Λόγος who are 'born of God' (ἐκ θεοῦ ἐγεννήθησαν, i. 12), and that such regeneration is the work of the Spirit in baptism (iii. 5). With all this in mind, we can see why the Jews who are hostile to Christ cannot maintain their claim to have God for their Father: they have not the capacity to hear the λόγος of Christ (43), or to recognize ἀλήθεια when it is spoken (45–7), which is tantamount to saying that they do not receive the Λόγος.[1]

---

the argument is certainly less effective rhetorically. The Jews are allowed to assume the validity of their descent from Abraham until inexorable logic fastens upon them the sinister ancestry of 44; ὑμεῖς ἐκ τοῦ πατρὸς τοῦ διαβόλου ἐστέ is surely intended to come like a thunderclap. Its force is weakened if already in 38 a non-Abrahamic ancestry has been asserted on the ground of their 'works'. Moreover, it would seem natural enough to speak of the Jews 'hearing' what they are to do from their father Abraham, as the original source of the immemorial oral tradition transmitted to his descendants (the reading ἑωράκατε in the second clause, found in D and other MSS. and in the Sinaitic Syriac, is probably by assimilation to ἑώρακα in the first clause). It may well be that those MSS. (including B) are right which omit the pronouns μου and ὑμῶν in the two clauses. There is not as yet any strong emphasis upon the different parentage of Christ and of the Jews: the point is that he behaves as a son should, truly representing his father; the Jews therefore should do the same. If they should understand him as meaning that he is a good son of Abraham and they are not, no harm would be done, at this stage of the argument, and it would be consistent with the Johannine irony. In 41 it is more difficult to take ποιεῖτε as imperative, though it may well be carried by the two previous occurrences of the same form. But perhaps here for the first time there is a suggestion of a 'father' who is not identical with Abraham, and this leads the Jews to make the more august claim, ἕνα πατέρα ἔχομεν τὸν θεόν.

[1] On this, see *Interpretation*, pp. 176–8, 265–8, 221–2.

Without going further into the details of the argument, we may fairly conclude (*a*) that in Jn. viii, as in Galatians, we are in contact with the 'Judaistic' controversy in the early Church, but (*b*) that the treatment of the matters of controversy is completely independent of Paul.[1] Here at any rate John is not 'deutero-Pauline'. The dialogue is in fact a highly original composition, strongly marked with the traits of the evangelist's diction, style and thought.

Indeed, if it seems probable that the dialogue has its roots in the 'Judaistic' controversy, it is far from being a mere broadsheet in the interests of one party to an ecclesiastical dispute. The genius of the Fourth Evangelist has lifted the whole argument (especially in the closing verses, 42–7, where the characteristic marks of his authorship are strongest) to a level where its local and temporary aspects recede, and the issues are universal and radical: truth and reality, the death-desires that spring from the lie and bring incapacity to hear the Word, and, finally, a man's ultimate relation to God. By this time we do not care greatly who the 'believing Jews' may have been, or what was their destiny. It is possible for others beside first-century 'Judaizers' to think that they 'believe', to boast of their 'freedom', to say with conviction (as Christians say every day) 'We have God for our Father'—and yet not to 'listen to the words of God'. John would have his readers consider such possibilities and face the consequences.

Do we not catch here echoes of an earlier tradition? 'Not everyone that saith unto me, "Lord, Lord", shall enter into the kingdom of heaven, but he that doeth the will of my Father in heaven' (Matt. vii. 21): the Synoptic Gospels offer much to that effect, and the ethos of it is strongly impressed upon the Johannine dialogue. Still clearer are the echoes of the passage in which Matthew (iii. 7–10) and Luke (iii. 7–9) report the preaching of John the Baptist, in terms so nearly identical that we must believe the passage to have been drawn by both from an earlier source. Here we are told that when the Baptist issued his call for repentance certain persons 'came to be baptized by

---

[1] As we have seen, the only close echo of Pauline language, δοῦλος τῆς ἁμαρτίας, is probably due to a scribe and not to the evangelist.

him' (according to Luke), or at least 'came to the baptism' (according to Matthew). They are therefore to be regarded as at least potential converts.[1] The Baptist's reception of them can hardly be described as cordial or conciliatory. His aim, it seems, is to shake their complacency. With this aim he warns them, μὴ δόξητε (or ἄρξησθε) λέγειν ἐν ἑαυτοῖς, Πατέρα ἔχομεν τὸν Ἀβραάμ. The potential converts, therefore, are represented as claiming the security given by descent from Abraham, in much the same sense, and in almost the same words, as the unsatisfactory 'believing Jews' of Jn. viii. 33. The Baptist deprecates the claim and demands moral conduct as the expression of a sincere intention: ποιήσατε καρπὸν (καρποὺς) ἄξιον (ἀξίους) τῆς μετανοίας. This alone, he implies, will entitle his potential converts to a place in the purified community which is being constituted by the 'baptism of repentance'. Without it, they are γεννήματα ἐχιδνῶν. As for children of Abraham, the Creator has ample power to supply them even if it means turning stones into men.[2]

We have here a very simple statement of the position which underlies the subtle and elaborate argument of Jn. viii. 31–47. There a group of professed 'believers', who are in some sort analogous to the group who came to be baptized by John, react to an offer which may be compared with John's offer of baptism on the basis of 'repentance', by declaring, σπέρμα

---

[1] According to Luke these persons were drawn from the general public (οἱ ὄχλοι); according to Matthew they were a numerous body of 'Pharisees and Sadducees'. One would suppose Luke's account to have more historical verisimilitude; yet Matthew's might have a certain contact with Jn. viii, if by Ἰουδαῖοι that evangelist means (as he often seems to mean) the governing class in Judaea.

[2] One cannot help thinking of Deucalion; but perhaps the Baptist had never heard of him! The Pauline way of putting it is to say that God 'calls things that are not as if they were' (Rom. iv. 17). That is, in fact, how God provided Abraham with his son Isaac, and there are many children of Abraham born, like Isaac, κατὰ πνεῦμα and not κατὰ σάρκα (Gal. iv. 29). The Johannine equivalent is the οὐκ ἐξ αἱμάτων οὐδὲ ἐκ θελήματος σαρκός οὐδὲ εκ θελήματος ἀνδρός ἀλλ' ἐκ θεοῦ, cf i. 13.

'Αβραὰμ ἐσμέν, ὁ πατὴρ ἡμῶν 'Αβραάμ ἐστιν. As the Baptist
brushed the claim aside and insisted, ποιήσατε καρπὸν ἄξιον
τῆς μετανοίας, so Jesus here retorts, εἰ τέκνα 'Αβραάμ ἐστε, τὰ
ἔργα τοῦ 'Αβραὰμ ποιεῖτε. Failing the fulfilment of this condition they are no better than children of the devil—which
is more explicit, but perhaps not substantially other, than
γεννήματα ἐχιδνῶν. In any case, they are not ἐκ τοῦ θεοῦ, and
for this evangelist that means that they are outside the realm
of 'truth', or reality, which is the redeemed order. Like the
devil himself, they have no standing ground in the realm of
reality (οὐχ ἕστηκεν[1] ἐν τῇ ἀληθείᾳ). All this is clothed in the
theological diction characteristic of the Fourth Evangelist, but
it was adumbrated in the plain and simple sayings in Matthew
and Luke which to all appearance belong to the most primitive
tradition.

The sayings we have been considering are attributed to John
the Baptist, and there is no reason to doubt the attribution.
But it seems clear that the primitive Church tradition preserved
sayings of the Baptist as an integral part of its tradition, along
with sayings of Jesus. It appears indeed that the distinction
between the two classes of sayings was not always rigidly
observed.[2] In any case there are sayings of Jesus which express

[1] MSS. vary between ἕστηκεν and ἑστηκεν. If the former reading
be accepted (imperfect from στήκω) the meaning would be, 'he did
not stand firm in the truth', implying that the devil was once within
the realm of ἀλήθεια but fell away. John however betrays no
interest in the doctrine of a primaeval fall of Satan, which in fact
seems excluded by the statement that he was a murderer ἀπ' ἀρχῆς.
The more probable reading is ἕστηκεν, the perfect of ἵστημι
normally used in the sense of a present: 'he does not stand in the
truth', i.e. he has no standing in the world of reality. MS. evidence is
not to be relied on where it is a question of breathings or aspirates.

[2] To this extent Bultmann, *Geschichte der synoptischen Tradition*,
p. 123 is right, though it is perhaps going too far to say that the
attribution of these sayings to John rather than to Jesus is 'blosser
Zufall'. It is, however, significant that γεννήματα ἐχιδνῶν κ.τ.λ. is
attributed to John in Matt. iii. 7, and to Jesus in xxiii. 33, and that
μετανοεῖτε, ἤγγικεν ἡ βασιλεία κ.τ.λ., which in Mk. i. 15 is a

the same standpoint as these of the Baptist. Thus in Matt. viii. 11–12 those who might expect to sit down with Abraham 'in the Kingdom of heaven', the υἱοὶ τῆς βασιλείας (= Israelites, the 'royal family', as it were, heirs of Abraham) are excluded, while their place is taken by strangers. And in the parable of Dives and Lazarus (Lk. xvi. 74–5) the rich man appeals to 'father Abraham', but although Abraham recognizes the relationship (τέκνον) this does not bring with it any alleviation of his lot. Son of Abraham he is, but not an heir of the kingdom promised to Abraham. Or as John would put it, he is σπέρμα Ἀβραάμ, but not ἐκ τοῦ θεοῦ.

It is a tempting conjecture (more than a conjecture it cannot be) that another saying belonging broadly to the same strain of tradition has found its way into the Matthaean 'anti-Pharisaic' discourse, xxiii. 9: πατέρα μὴ καλέσητε ἐπὶ τῆς γῆς· εἷς γὰρ ἐστιν ὑμῶν ὁ πατὴρ ὁ οὐράνιος. The latter part of this saying looks like an echo of Malachi ii. 10: οὐχὶ θεὸς εἷς ἔκτισεν ὑμᾶς; οὐχὶ πατὴρ εἷς πάντων ὑμῶν; This is also echoed in Jn. viii. 41, ἕνα πατέρα ἔχομεν τὸν θεόν (which in the turn of phrase resembles Matt. iii. 9, πατέρα ἔχομεν τὸν Ἀβραάμ). The saying fits oddly into its Matthaean context, being sandwiched between two sayings which we must surely regard as doublets: verse 8, μη κληθῆτε ῥαββεί κ.τ.λ., and verse 10, μὴ κληθῆτε καθηγηταί κ.τ.λ.[1] The prohibition of honorific titles among the disciples of Jesus is quite in place after a denunciation of the 'scribes and Pharisees' for delighting in such titles. If verse 9 had read 'Do not be called "father",' it would have fitted reasonably well; apparently the title 'Abba' was sometimes given to distinguished rabbis[2] and the disciples might well be forbidden to accept it. But it is not so clear what would be meant in such a context by the precept that the disciples

---

prophetic word of Jesus, is in Matt. iii. 2 given (almost certainly wrongly) to John.

[1] Verse 8 would be drawn from a tradition preserved in circles which still understood the Jewish title Rabbi, verse 10 from a tradition adapted to Greek-speaking circles for whom it needed to be translated.

[2] See Strack-Billerbeck *ad loc.*

are not to *give* the title to anyone on earth. It would be in line with Matthew's practice to supply a more or less appropriate context to a saying which was handed down as an independent aphorism. If this is an instance, we may legitimately enquire into the meaning of the saying without regard to its setting in the gospel as it stands.[1] Now there is a *baraita* (in *Berachoth* 16, cited by Strack-Billerbeck *ad loc.*) which says 'One calls "father" none but the Three' (*scil*: Abraham, Isaac and Jacob). It is perhaps not too wild a conjecture that the saying before us was intended to mean, 'Call no earthly being "father" —*not even Abraham*—since you all have one Father in heaven'.[2] This would be another way of saying, μὴ δόξητε λέγειν ἐν ἑαυτοῖς, πατέρα ἔχομεν τὸν Ἀβραάμ. If so, then Jn. viii. 39–42 carries the matter one step further. To say, ὁ πατὴρ ἡμῶν Ἀβραάμ ἐστιν, is beside the point, unless it is accompanied by ἔργα τοῦ Ἀβραάμ. Not only so, to say πατέρα ἔχομεν τὸν θεόν may provoke the severest condemnation of all, unless those who make the claim are truly ἐκ τοῦ θεοῦ, and show it by 'hearing the word of God' (verse 4), which gives knowledge of ἀλήθεια and so brings the liberty which descent from Abraham cannot guarantee.

To sum up, our study has pointed towards some such conclusion as this: the dialogue is related to the episode of the 'Judaistic' controversy in the early Church, but it turns upon ideas which were not first struck out under the impact of that controversy, or given currency by Paul, its protagonist, but belong to the earliest strata of the Gospel tradition. Here and,

[1] It is hardly likely to be a call for the renunciation of family ties in the sense of Matt. x. 37, Lk. xiv. 26, Mk. x. 29, or of Matt. viii. 22 = Lk. ix. 59. The motive for such renunciation is devotion to Christ and his cause, not our common brotherhood in the family of God.

[2] The fatherhood of God is contrasted with the fatherhood of Abraham, though with a different intention, in Isa. lxiii. 16, 'Thou art our father, though Abraham knoweth us not, and Israel doth not acknowledge us: thou, O Lord, art our father; our redeemer from everlasting is thy name' (the LXX has missed the meaning here).

I believe, elsewhere the Fourth Evangelist has reached back to the primitive testimony, by-passing in large measure the theological development associated with the name of Paul, to find a solid basis for his own theological interpretation of the Gospel.

5 The Prophecy of Caiaphas: John xi. 47–53

The passage to be considered, while it purports to recount an historical incident, has also (*more Johanneo*) theological content. The significance attaching to it in the great argument of the Fourth Gospel is apparent from the position which the evangelist has given to it. In xi. 1–44 Christ is set forth as the Resurrection and the Life, who gives life to dead Lazarus. In order to do so, he enters the place where his own life is in danger (xi. 8, 16); the evangelist, after his manner, hints that Christ must die in order to give life to men. This theme is elaborated in the discourse, xii. 23–33, ending with the words, τοῦτο δὲ ἔλεγεν σημαίνων ποίῳ θανάτῳ ἔμελλεν ἀποθνῄσκειν, and thus the way is prepared for the Passion narrative which is to follow. The intervening passages make the transition. In xi. 47–53 Jesus is devoted to death by the authorities of his nation. In xii. 1–8 he is anointed for burial. His final triumph (after death) is symbolized by his acclamation as King of Israel, which (says the evangelist) was a tribute to his victory over death in the raising of Lazarus.[1] The short *pericopé*, therefore, with which we are concerned, has profound theological significance. It not only establishes the fact that Jesus is to die, but it also states the purpose and the effect of his dying: he dies 'to gather into one the scattered children of God'. Similarly in xii. 32 by dying Christ will draw all men to himself, and in x. 15–16 (by clear implication if not *totidem verbis*) he dies to bring in his other sheep, not of this (the Jewish) fold, so that there may be one flock as there is one Shepherd. Our *pericopé* therefore brings us near to the centre of Johannine theology. We are in the presence of one of the most characteristic and distinctive ideas of this evangelist, without precise parallel elsewhere in the New Testament.[2]

[1] See C. H. Dodd, *The Interpretation of the Fourth Gospel*, pp. 366–371.

[2] The idea that the great eschatological Event (however con-

But the words in which this idea is expressed, ἵνα καὶ τὰ τέκνα τοῦ θεοῦ . . . συναγάγῃ εἰς ἕν (52), are introduced as a corollary to a proposition which is very far from suggesting any such idea: ἔμελλεν Ἰησοῦς ἀποθνήσκειν ὑπὲρ τοῦ ἔθνους (51). The transitional phrase, οὐχ ὑπὲρ τοῦ ἔθνους μόνον, is obviously designed to give the desired turn—a quite arbitrary turn—to a maxim which is not itself congenial to this evangelist. It is therefore improbable in the extreme that the composition of the *pericopé* is the original work of the writer who added the corollary (the writer whose theology dominates the whole work). He must be supposed to have received, from some source or other, the account of the prophecy of Caiaphas, and to have turned it adroitly to account by the introduction of the words of verse 52. What then was the source from which he drew this remarkable account? Even the most resolute advocate of the view that John was dependent on the Synoptics will hardly argue seriously that Jn. xi. 47–53 is an expansion of Matt. xxvi. 3–5, although that passage contains the name Caiaphas and the words ἐβουλεύσαντο ἵνα . . . ἀποκτείνωσιν, which occur also in John. It seems that we must look elsewhere.

We may first see whether anything can be learnt from the structure or pattern of the passage, assuming that it ended (before it was handled by our evangelist) with verse 51. It has a certain general resemblance to a class of *pericopae* in the Synoptic Gospels for which perhaps the best label is Vincent Taylor's 'pronouncement story', since that is descriptive and comprehensive and begs no question. Like other *pericopae* of the class it opens with a concise setting of the scene (συνήγαγον οἱ ἀρχιερεῖς καὶ οἱ φαρισαῖοι συνέδριον). A brief dialogue follows (47–8), and this leads up to a pregnant saying (50), to which is annexed an interpretative comment (52).[1] So far, the

---

ceived) includes the gathering of the people of God (Israel, or the elect) has deep roots; Isa. xi. 12, xliii. 5 *et passim*, Ezek. xxviii. 25, etc., Mk. xiii. 27, II Thess. ii. 1; but the close connection of this with the death of Christ is specifically Johannine.

[1] Cf. Mk. ii. 15–17, 18–20, 24–8, iii. 31–5, ix. 33–5, x. 13–16, xii. 13–17; Lk. xiii. 31–3.

passage looks like a fairly typical unit of tradition, and it contrasts with this writer's more usual manner. It would be a
reasonable hypothesis that he is here incorporating a piece of
tradition more or less as it reached him. This hypothesis must
now be tested.

The passage is exceptional in that the pregnant saying is not
uttered by Jesus, who indeed is absent from the whole scene.
In the Synoptic Gospels there is no 'pronouncement story' in
which a speaker other than Jesus utters the pronouncement for
the sake of which the story is told, and there is no scene
between the Baptism and the Crucifixion in which he is not
the central figure—with one exception, the death of the Baptist
in Mk. vi. 17–29. Other exceptions are apparent rather than
real. The account of the proceedings of the hierarchy in
Mk. xiv. 1–2, and of their corrupt compact with Judas in
xiv. 10–11 (originally, probably, continuous, but separated by
Mark's characteristic method of 'sandwiching') has nothing of
the form of a traditional unit of narrative; it is simply part of
the introduction to the Passion narrative, and is similar in
character to the *Sammelberichte* which often serve to connect
narrative *pericopae*.[1] The little paragraph about Herod's judgment on Jesus in Mk. vi. 14–16 is in no sense an independent
unit; it serves merely as introduction to the passage about the

---

[1] The verbs ἐζήτουν, ἔλεγον (1–2), are in the 'continuous' tense,
as is usual in such summary passages, describing the situation as it
was over a period rather than any particular incident. The treachery
of Judas is recorded in aorists, but the passage again reverts to the
imperfect ἐζήτει in 11 to describe the situation as it was after that
fatal step had been taken. Matt. xxvi. 3–5 has substituted for Mark's
summary with verbs in the imperfect a narrative with verbs in the
aorist, but these verbs, be it observed, come out of Ps. xxx (xxxi).
14 (a *testimonium* which may also have influenced the language of
Jn. xi. 47, 53). The use of testimonies, and the introduction of the
proper name, may point to development in oral *didaché* rather than
to a mere 'editing' of Mark. But the passage can hardly be described
as a typical narrative unit, to the extent to which that description
would fit the Johannine *pericopé*.

death of the Baptist.[1] So far as the Synoptic Gospels are concerned we may fairly say that such a unit as appears to lie behind Jn. xi. 47–53 would be alien to the tradition which they follow, in spite of a general resemblance of form.

Then is there any evidence to suggest that the Fourth Evangelist worked with a tradition which, while broadly similar in formation, did not adhere so rigidly to the canon which appears to have governed the formation of the Synoptic tradition, viz. that at all times Jesus should be clearly portrayed in speech or action? Certainly there are several scenes in which Jesus does not appear in person. In iv. 28–9, 41–2, the Samaritan woman converses with her fellow-townsmen in the absence of Jesus; in vii. 40–52, xi. 56–7, the Jerusalem public and the authorities discuss his claims; but in neither case have we anything remotely resembling the compact unit of narrative which has been noted in xi. 47–51. The dissimilarity is the more marked because vii. 47–52 and xi. 47–51 both deal with a judgment upon Jesus by the Jewish authorities, but in widely different ways. The passages referred to are examples of a typically Johannine technique: a dramatic scene is distributed between two stages (as it were);[2] comment on the back stage elucidates action on the front stage. More important is the long and elaborate trial scene of ix. 13–34, in which Jesus does not appear at all. But this is in any case unlike any other passage in the gospels, and there is nothing to compare it with; it has no resemblance to the passage we are considering. It is only in the *coda*, ix. 39–41, where Jesus appears in order to dismiss the whole scene with a pregnant saying, that we have once again something approximating to a traditional unit.

There remains the passage, iii. 25–30, which has something of the aspect of a traditional 'pronouncement story'. The scene

[1] It has been surmised that vi. 14–15 is a mere duplicate of viii. 28, and that vi. 16 was originally the introduction to a story about what Herod did. But all this is conjecture. No doubt there has been a good deal of editorial work hereabouts, but in any case vi. 14–16 provides no exception to the rule that in narrative *pericopae* in the Synoptic Gospels Jesus always speaks or acts.

[2] See C. H. Dodd, *Interpretation of the Fourth Gospel*, pp. 347–8.

is concisely laid: ἐγένετο ζήτησις κ.τ.λ. (25). A brief dialogue
follows, leading up to a parable (29) which is interpreted in
a pregnant saying, ἐκεῖνον δεῖ αὐξάνειν ἐμὲ δὲ ἐλαττοῦσθαι
(30). In spite of some elaboration in obviously Johannine language, this might well be accepted as a not impossible unit
of tradition of typical form. But the pregnant saying is attributed to the Baptist and not to Jesus. However, it seems clear
that the primitive tradition did contain sayings of John the
Baptist as well as sayings of Jesus, and there is no reason why
iii. 23–9 should not have come down by such tradition. But
we are still very far from a real parallel to xi. 47–52, where the
pregnant saying to which the dialogue leads up is assigned to
an enemy of Jesus, and yet is accepted as an important doctrinal
pronouncement, and accepted not only by the evangelist (in
an arbitrary sense), but also, it appears, already in the story as
it reached him.

The conclusion appears to be that while we cannot safely
attribute the passage we are considering to the general body
of oral tradition, which, so far as we know it, is shaped by the
motive of presenting Jesus himself in significant speech and
action, yet the form it has taken does seem to imply some
affinity with that tradition, sufficient, perhaps, to encourage an
enquiry into a possible *milieu* in which it might have taken
shape.

The passage culminates in the pronouncement, συμφέρει
ὑμῖν ἵνα εἷς ἄνθρωπος ἀποθάνῃ ὑπὲρ τοῦ λαοῦ καὶ μὴ ὅλον τὸ
ἔθνος ἀπόληται. It is in form a general maxim: the sacrifice of an
individual is never too high a price to pay for national security.
But this is immediately given a precise application (the application obviously indicated by the context): ὅτι ἔμελλεν Ἰησοῦς
ἀποθνῇσκειν ὑπὲρ τοῦ ἔθνους. (The words following, καὶ οὐχ
ὑπὲρ τοῦ ἔθνους μόνον, as we have seen, are a part of the
evangelist's 're-interpretation' of the saying.) The death of
Jesus is regarded as a means by which the Jewish nation may
be saved from disaster; it is a λύτρον for Israel. It is the same
conception that underlies Mk. x. 45, only treated in a purely
secular spirit, and looked at from the opposite side: in Mark
the λύτρον is willingly offered, in the pronouncement of Caiaphas it is exacted by means of a judicial murder; whereas

in Mark it is (vaguely) ἀντὶ πολλῶν, in John it is (precisely) ὑπὲρ τοῦ ἔθνους.[1] So Caiaphas says; but what is more important is that the comment, from the authority (whoever he may have been) for the form of tradition which John follows, accepts the statement: Jesus was indeed to die for Israel—no doubt in a more profound sense than Caiaphas dreamed of, but still, ὑπὲρ τοῦ ἔθνους. In what circle was the λύτρον-concept of the death of Christ likely to be thus restricted to Israel? It can hardly have been other than a Jewish Christian circle still acutely conscious of its solidarity with the 'commonwealth of Israel' as a whole.

But we have yet to consider the most remarkable feature of the passage: the pregnant utterance of Caiaphas is inspired prophecy, for Caiaphas, ἀρχιερεὺς ὤν . . ., ἐπροφήτευσεν. The implication, no doubt, is that he spoke more truly than he knew; he was prophesying without being aware of it. Unconscious prophecy is recognized in Jewish sources cited by Strack-Billerbeck *ad loc.* But that is a minor matter. Whether consciously or unconsciously, the high priest is a prophet *jure dignitatis*: this is an essential element in the passage as it came down to the evangelist.

The priest is also prophet: commentators cite in illustration Philo, *De Spec. Leg.* IV. 192, ὁ πρὸς ἀλήθειαν ἱερεὺς εὐθύς ἐστι προφήτης. It will be well to complete the quotation: ὁ πρὸς ἀλήθειαν ἱερεὺς εὐθύς ἐστι προφήτης, οὐ γένει μᾶλλον ἢ ἀρετῇ παρεληλυθὼς ἐπὶ τὴν τοῦ ὄντος θεραπείαν, προφήτῃ δὲ οὐδὲν ἄγνωστον, ἔχοντι νοητὸν ἥλιον ἐν ἑαυτῷ καὶ ἀσκίους αὐγάς, εἰς ἐναργεστάτην κατάληψιν τῶν αἰσθήσει μὲν ἀοράτων διανοίᾳ δέ καταληπτῶν. Philo is speaking, not of empirical priesthood, such as that of the temple at Jerusalem, but of ideal priesthood, *scil.* that of the enlightened soul able to contemplate the κόσμος νοητός. The perfect example of such

---

[1] Πολλοί is vague; there is nothing to show whether (in the tradition behind Mark) it was conceived to include Gentiles or only the totality of Israel. Nor does reference to Isa. liii. 11-12 settle the question, for various interpretations are possible, according as the Servant is thought of as an individual or as the nation (or its faithful remnant) collectively.

priesthood is Moses, who by divine providence became βασιλεύς τε καὶ νομοθέτης καὶ ἀρχιερεὺς καὶ προφήτης (*De Vit. Mos.* II. 3); who possessed four prerogatives, τέταρτον δὲ ἀρχιερωσύνην δι᾿ ἧς προφητεύων ἐπιστημονικῶς θεραπεύσει τὸ ὄν (*De Praem.* 53–6 *et simm. passim*). In this Moses is a type of the Logos: ὁ προφήτης λόγος, ὄνομα Μωυσῆς (*De Congressu* 170 *et alibi*). The Logos is the true priest-prophet: προστέτακται τῷ ἱερεῖ καὶ προφήτῃ λόγῳ τὴν ψυχὴν ἐναντίον τοῦ θεοῦ στῆσαι ἀποκαλύφῳ τῇ κεφαλῇ (*De Cher.* 17, referring to Num. v. 19). These are only a few out of numerous passages in Philo to similar effect. It is clear that our present passage is moving in a different world of thought. There is no hint here of the Logos doctrine; nothing about contemplation of the unseen or worship of τὸ ὄν: it is no ideal priest-prophet that utters the oracle in Jn. xi. 50; it is the all too earthy Caiaphas, high priest in Jerusalem under Pontius Pilate. Nor is it the evangelist, with a philosophy akin to Philo's, who speaks here; it is a tradition much nearer to popular Judaism.

There is evidence that in popular belief prophetic powers were associated with the office of high priest. Josephus tells the story that when Alexander the Great was approaching Jerusalem and there was panic in the city, the High Priest Jaddua received an oracle in a dream: ἐχρημάτισεν αὐτῷ κατὰ τοὺς ὕπνους ὁ θεὸς θαρρεῖν καὶ στεφανοῦντας τὴν πόλιν ἀνοίγειν τὰς πύλας καὶ . . . ποιεῖσθαι τὴν ὑπάντησιν μηδὲν προσδοκοῦντας πείσεσθαι δεινόν. And so it turned out: Alexander received the high priest with all honour (*Antiq.* xi. 327 sqq.). Hyrcanus, again, was at once civil ruler, prophet and high priest: τρίων τῶν μεγίστων ἄξιος ὑπὸ τοῦ θεοῦ κριθείς, ἀρχῆς τοῦ ἔθνους καὶ τῆς ἀρχιερατικῆς τιμῆς καὶ προφητείας. As prophet he foresaw the future and predicted the fortunes of his two eldest sons (*ibid.*, xiii. 299–300). Josephus indeed himself pretended to prophetic powers,[1] and apparently he thought, or at least wished his readers to think, that this was an attribute of the priestly character which he possessed by descent. He does not actually say so; what he does say is that as a priest he was familiar with Old Testament prophecy, and

[1] *B.J.* iii. 351, 399–408.

that this in some way enabled him to interpret the oracular dreams with which he was favoured—very conveniently favoured, since they furnished an apology for his defection to the Romans in the Jewish War.[1] We need not take all this too seriously, but in the background hovers the belief that prophecy and priesthood went together. That prophecy might be expected of a high priest, in particular, is confirmed also by a passage (cited by Schlatter, *Der Evangelist Johannes, ad loc.*) in *Tosephta Sota* 13, 5–6, referring to Hyrcanus and Simon the Just. We are therefore justified in concluding that the words of Jn. xi. 51, ἀρχιερεὺς ὢν ἐπροφήτευσεν, echo a popular belief of first-century Judaism.

It would appear, then, that the circle in which the tradition represented by Jn. xi. 47–51 was handed down stood very close to Jewish circles in which this belief was alive. A Christian circle it must have been, in which a saying which could be taken as expressing the interpretation of the death of Jesus as λύτρον was welcome. Equally clearly it was Jewish, for such a valuation of the office of high priest, even when its occupant was unworthy, could hardly have persisted among Christians already aware of a distance between them and the Jewish community. The words of Caiaphas are accepted as true prophecy, and this is taken so seriously that they occupy the place in a 'pronouncement story' which is normally given to a *Herrnwort*. Behind all this we seem to discern an early Palestinian Jewish Christianity still within the body of the Jewish nation, and

---

[1] *B.J.* III. 352–3: ἦν δὲ καὶ περὶ κρίσεις ὀνείρων ἱκανὸς συμβαλεῖν τὰ ἀμφιβόλως ὑπὸ τοῦ θείου λεγόμενα· τῶν γε μὴν ἱερῶν βίβλων οὐκ ἠγνόει τὰς προφητείας ὡς ἂν αὐτὸς τ᾽ ὢν ἱερεὺς καὶ ἱερέων ἔγγονος, ὧν ἐπὶ τῆς τόθ᾽ ὥρας ἔνθους γενόμενος καὶ τὰ φρικώδη τῶν προσφάτων ὀνείρων σπάσας φαντάσματα προσφέρει τῷ θεῷ λεληθυῖαν εὐχήν—in which he professed, ὡς οὐ προδότης ἀλλὰ σὸς ἄπειμι διάκονος. The inspiration of the moment came (if we construe the genitive in the only way which seems possible with ἔνθους) out of the scriptures with which he was familiar. But the language seems studiously inexplicit. He clearly wished to suggest, without actually saying it, that as a priest he had experience of prophetic inspiration.

sharing in general its beliefs and religious attitudes, including the *mystique* of the Jerusalem priesthood and temple, which in the main line of Christian thought faded rapidly before the concept of the spiritual temple and the high priesthood of Christ.

Such is the inference to which we seem to be led by an examination of the crucial pronouncement in which the passage culminates. We may further ask whether there is anything inconsistent with such a *provenance* for the *pericopé* as a whole. That there should be traces of re-writing in the author's highly individual style is to be expected. There are few passages in the gospel, whatever their sources may have been, which do not in this way betray the hand of the evangelist. But the Johannine stamp on the language of this passage is not in any case deep, and in fact two significant terms, λογίζεσθαι and προφητεύειν are, as it happens, ἅπαξ λεγόμενα in the Johannine writings. But the locutions ποιεῖν σημεῖα, πιστεύειν εἰς,[1] ἀφ᾽ ἑαυτοῦ,[2] are characteristic of this author. The expression

---

[1] *Ποιεῖν σημεῖα*, 14 times in John, not elsewhere in the gospels. *Πιστεύειν εἰς* extremely common in John, once only in Synoptics, Matt. xviii. 6 (and as f.l. in Mk. ix. 42). So far, therefore, the comments of members of the Sanhedrin are clearly of Johannine mintage. Is the continuation ἐλεύσονται οἱ ῾Ρωμαῖοι καὶ ἀροῦσιν ἡμῶν καὶ τὸν τόπον (*scil.* the temple) καὶ τὸ ἔθνος, also to be assigned to the evangelist, who knew that in A.D. 70 the Romans had destroyed the temple and abolished the Jewish national state? Possibly, but it is not necessarily a case of 'hindsight'. It did not require special inspiration to see whither things were tending during the last half-century before the great rebellion, and in fact it is clear from Josephus's account that the hierarchy was constantly apprehensive of the consequences that might ensue if the 'national resistance movement' were given its head. Josephus calls the 'resistance fighters' λῃσταί, and according to Mk. xiv. 48 Jesus protested that he was being treated as a λῃστής.

[2] ᾽Αφ᾽ ἑαυτοῦ, six times in John, mostly with λέγειν, εἰπεῖν, λαλεῖν, once in Luke (ἀφ᾽ ἑαυτῶν, xii. 57), as f.l. in Acts xxi. 23, otherwise unknown in N.T. Perhaps ἀφ᾽ ἑαυτοῦ οὐκ εἶπεν (= he spoke by divine inspiration) is the evangelist's paraphrase of ἐπροφήτευσεν.

ἀρχιερεὺς τοῦ ἐνιαυτοῦ ἐκείνου, which occurs also in xviii. 13, must probably be put to his account. It appears on the face of it to imply that the high priesthood at Jerusalem was, like many priesthoods in Greek cities, an annual appointment.[1] This would scarcely be possible in any early Palestinian Jewish source, though the rapidity with which some Roman governors transferred the office might excuse the mistake in a writer working, at a distance, on material received, without personal experience of conditions before the fall of the temple. Similarly the use of the term φαρισαῖοι, as if it denoted an 'estate' of the Sanhedrin, collateral with the ἀρχιερεῖς, seems to imply a misconception which runs all through this gospel. The Pharisees formed a voluntary association, or group of associations (חבורות), for the furtherance of certain religious principles, and these had no standing as an organ of constitutional government or administration. Possibly our evangelist confused φαρισαῖοι with γραμματεῖς. Most γραμματεῖς, apparently, though certainly not all, were in fact adherents of the Pharisaic party, and γραμματεῖς *were* an 'estate' of the Sanhedrin. But the misconception could hardly have arisen in an early Palestinian Jewish environment.

If we make so much allowance for re-handling, there does not appear to be any cogent reason against the *prima facie* conclusion that we have here, substantially, material which goes back to early Jewish Christianity. There are in various places of this gospel some further hints that the author was drawing upon material of this kind.

(i) It is significant that among the predictions of persecution in store for the disciples of Jesus, which have a place in all gospels, the Fourth Gospel has nothing parallel to the Synoptic forecasts of trials before βασιλεῖς καὶ ἡγεμόνες (i.e. provincial governors), or of witness to the Gentiles.[2] They must be prepared for death at the hands of those who believe themselves to be serving God, i.e. fellow-Jews. Next to death, the worst they have to fear is expulsion from the synagogue[3]—a fate

---

[1] Attempts to evade this implication I find more ingenious than convincing.

[2] Matt. x. 18; Mk. xiii. 9–10; Lk. xxi. 12.   [3] Jn. xvi. 2.

which would hold no terrors for any but Jewish Christians, and such of them as valued their continued membership of the Jewish community.

(ii) The account of the examination of Jesus before the high priest (xviii. 19–23), unlike that in Mark (xiv. 53–64), is entirely non-theological in character. There is nothing about the threat to destroy the temple,[1] nothing about messianic claims, nothing about blasphemy. The high priest simply interrogates his Prisoner περὶ τῶν μαθητῶν αὐτοῦ καὶ περὶ τῆς διδαχῆς αὐτοῦ. This fits in well with the account given in *Bab. Sanh.* 43, that Jesus was condemned because he 'enticed' and 'led astray' Israel (הסית והדיח את ישראל). The verbs ות and נדח are those employed in Deut. iv. 19, xiii. 7, xxx. 17 of inducement to idolatry. According to the official Jewish tradition, therefore, Jesus was arraigned as a false teacher who was leading people to apostasy. If so, then it was quite in order for the high priest to investigate the nature of his teaching and the extent of his following.

(iii) The same tractate dates the execution of Jesus to the Eve of Passover (ערב הפסח) which is exactly represented by παρασκευὴ τοῦ πάσχα in Jn. xix. 14.[2] The date notoriously conflicts with that of the Synoptics. Whether rightly or wrongly, an identical date is given by the Fourth Gospel and by the tractate *Sanhedrin*, representing Jewish tradition on the subject.

The list might be extended.[3] The conclusion seems to be justified, that the Fourth Evangelist was in a position to draw, directly or indirectly, upon a source of information deriving from a very early Jewish Christian circle still in close association with the synagogue.

[1] In Mk. xiv. 57–8 the false witnesses quote an alleged saying of Jesus in which he threatens to destroy the temple. In Jn. ii. 19 he offers to restore the temple after its (hypothetical) destruction. The latter version of the saying is perhaps more likely to have come down by a tradition formed in a Jewish Christian environment where reverence for the temple was still alive.

[2] Attempts to make this mean something else, e.g. 'Friday in Passover', are unconvincing.

[3] See C. H. Dodd, *Historical Tradition in the Fourth Gospel,* pp. 435–6.

6 The Fall of Jerusalem and the 'Abomination of Desolation'

The Gospel according to Luke contains two passages which allude, with some particularity, to a forthcoming siege and destruction of Jerusalem; viz. xix. 42–4, xxi. 20–4.

The latter of these two passages (with which we may conveniently begin) stands in a context where Luke, to all appearance, is using the Gospel according to Mark as a source. The Marcan parallel to Lk. xxi. 20–4 forms part of what is often called the 'Synoptic Apocalypse', or, more appropriately, the 'Apocalyptic Discourse', since its literary form is not that of an apocalypse; it is in the main a *Mahnrede* making use of apocalyptic motives, and concluding with a few sentences of straightforward prediction in the apocalyptic manner (xiii. 24–7).

The prevailing critical view is that Mk. xiii. 5–27 represents either an early Christian apocalypse which Mark took over with little or no change, or a Jewish apocalypse which he has supplemented with Christian material. Luke, it is generally held, re-edited and in part re-wrote the Marcan discourse in the light of historical events which took place between the original composition of the 'apocalypse' and the time at which his gospel was written. That the Third Gospel was in fact produced after the Fall of Jerusalem is on other grounds fairly certain, while the Gospel according to Mark, or if not that gospel in its present form at least the bulk of the material in the Apocalyptic Discourse, may reasonably be dated to the period before the war of A.D. 66–70. 'It seems clear' (wrote J. M. Creed in his commentary on the Gospel, 1930, *ad. loc.*) 'that for Luke the fall of Jerusalem is past history. The contemporary situation has made it necessary for Luke to impose an interpretation upon his source which will distinguish for his readers between fulfilled and unfulfilled prophecy. This accounts for the main changes in Luke.' Our present passage, he continues, has been 'drastically edited. The "abomination of desolation" standing where it ought not is replaced by "Jerusalem encircled with armies". The fall of Jerusalem fulfils prophecy and the consequent dispersion of the Jews introduces the next epoch, "the times of the Gentiles", in which the evangelist and his readers live.' This may be said to be still the dominant view, though there have always been some critics who have allowed for the use of another source or sources as well as Mark.

Recent trends in criticism seem to call for a more radical reconsideration of the question than it has (to my knowledge) yet received. In the first place, it would be very generally admitted that the earlier 'Two-document Hypothesis' oversimplified the Synoptic Problem, and that the assumption (in particular) of the unconditional priority of Mark in passages where the gospels run parallel requires much qualification. Further, the method of *Formgeschichte* has led us to recognize that much of the material of the gospels was handed down orally (and perhaps even in writing) in the form of detached units of narrative and discourse. These units of tradition were built up by the evangelists (or their predecessors) into apparently continuous narratives and discourses, but the original discontinuity is often patent to careful observation. The separate units of tradition had a history of their own in the pre-canonical stage, and developed variations which may be reflected in the variations of the canonical record. Consequently, while the use of written sources (extant or conjectural), sometimes copied, sometimes 'edited' with greater or less freedom, is one explanation of the curious phenomena of agreement and difference which constitute the data of the Synoptic Problem, it is not necessarily an exhaustive explanation.

From this point of view the Apocalyptic Discourse appears as a sequence of warnings, precepts, and predictions, some of which are doublets of passages occurring in other parts of the gospels, while others readily separate themselves into typical units of tradition. Mk. xiii. 14–20, with which we are immediately concerned, is an oracle concerning the appearance of the 'Abomination of Desolation', with its immediate sequel, and is so far complete in itself. It is, however, itself composite.

Verses 15–16 are a doublet of Lk. xvii. 31, and may be supposed to have had a pre-canonical history outside their present context. Verses 19–20 may be regarded as comment or reflection upon the events in view in 14–18. It may well be that these diverse elements had already been welded together in the pre-canonical stage. But the connection of the whole episode with what precedes and what follows is not so organic that we are driven to conclude that this connection is original. Indeed, any attempt to define the chronological relations of this episode, before and after, reveals how disjointed the whole arrangement is.

The corresponding section of the Lucan discourse, xxi. 20–4, separates itself out equally clearly as a relatively complete oracle. But while its place in the general scheme of the discourse compels us to regard it as parallel to Mk. 14–18 (20), it is very different in character from the Marcan *pericopé*, and whereas in the preceding verses of Lk. (xxi. 8–19) there are, in spite of divergences, continuous echoes of Marcan language, verses 20–4 have not the slightest verbal resemblance to Mark except (i) 21*a* and 23*a*, which repeat Mark *verbatim*, and (ii) 20, where the general structure of the sentence, with the clause ὅταν δὲ ἴδητε and the single words τότε and ἐρήμωσις, appears to echo Mk. xiii. 14.

If for the moment we ignore these echoes of Marcan language we observe that verses 21*b*–22, 23*b*–24 form a homogeneous whole—far more homogeneous in *form* (to the content we shall come in a moment) than Mk. xiii. 15–18. These verses consist of a sequence of rhythmical couplets, displaying a fairly regular parallelism of the kind characteristic of Hebrew poetry. Verse 20, though it does not display parallelism, yet fits rhythmically into the same scheme. Are we to say that this homogeneous pattern is merely the result of Luke's 'editing' of his Marcan source? The term 'editing' is in fact inapplicable. In 21*b*–22, 23*b*–24 Luke is *either* following a different source, *or* writing 'out of his own head'. In 21*a*, 23*a* he is not 'editing' Mark, but simply copying him. It is only in 20 that it is plausible to speak of him as 'editing' Mk. xiii. 14. Is he in fact doing so?

Before attempting to answer this question it will be well to look at the sentences in which Marcan language is reproduced

exactly, 21*a*, 23*a*. There are reasons for supposing that these
are insertions into a previously existing pattern. (i) As we have
already observed, both break up a scheme of rhythm and
parallelism which is otherwise continuous. (ii) The clause,
τότε οἱ ἐν τῇ Ἰουδαίᾳ φευγέτωσαν εἰς τὰ ὄρη, is in Mark the
apodosis to the clause beginning ὅταν ἴδητε. In Luke it
is no longer so: that clause already has its own apodosis;
the second τότε in asyndeton hangs awkwardly in the air.
(iii) It is generally agreed by commentators that αὐτῆς and
αὐτήν in 21*b* must refer to Jerusalem. In ancient warfare it was
the custom for the rural population to take refuge within the
city walls on the appearance of enemy troops. In the special
circumstances here contemplated the rural population (οἱ ἐν
ταῖς χώραις) are enjoined *not* to do so. But as the sentence
stands, αὐτῆς and αὐτήν should refer to Ἰουδαία. It would
then mean that inhabitants of other districts or provinces
should not enter Judaea while the Roman armies are in
occupation—which seems unnecessary advice. If this argument
is sound, it not only shows the clause τότε οἱ ἐν τῇ Ἰουδαίᾳ
φευγέτωσαν εἰς τὰ ὄρη to be an intrusion, but shows also that
21*b* must originally have been the direct sequel, if not of 20 as
it now stands, at least of some similar statement which named
Jerusalem and indicated the ground upon which the rural
population is forbidden to follow the usual practice, viz.
because Jerusalem is doomed.

This brings us back to verse 20, where Luke is supposed to
be 'editing' Mark in the light of historical happenings known
to him but not to Mark. It will hardly be argued that the mere
expression, κυκλουμένην ὑπὸ στρατοπέδων, describes Titus's
siege so precisely that it must necessarily be a *vaticinium ex
eventu*. If you want to say in Greek 'Jerusalem will be besieged',
the choice of available expressions is strictly limited, and
κυκλοῦσθαι ὑπὸ στρατοπέδων is about as colourless as any.
But, it is urged, the choice of the term ἐρήμωσις must surely
have been dictated by Mark's τὸ βδέλυγμα τῆς ἐρημώσεως,
which Luke wished to modify because it would be unintelligible
to the public he had in view. But in fact the choice of the term
ἐρήμωσις is most natural for anyone whose thought and
language are coloured by reminiscences of the Greek Old

Testament—that is for any Greek-speaking Jew or Christian of the period. The extent to which Luke's language is so coloured I shall illustrate presently. Here it will be well to exhibit at once some of the evidence for ἐρήμωσις.

The word ἐρήμωσις (rendering two different Hebrew words of similar meaning) is not uncommon in the Septuagint. For our purpose it is significant that it occurs frequently in the Book of Jeremiah, where the prophet has occasion to speak of the national débâcle which he saw approaching and of which he was in the end a witness. Thus, in one of his earliest prophecies he describes the impending attack of an enemy from the north (the Scythians, it is supposed), whose advance will leave a trail of devastation behind it: ἐξῆλθεν ἐκ τοῦ τόπου αὐτοῦ τοῦ θεῖναι τὴν γῆν εἰς ἐρήμωσιν¹, καὶ πόλεις καθαιρεθήσονται παρὰ τὸ κατοικεῖσθαι αὐτάς (iv. 7). Later, he pronounces the doom of the Temple, which has become a σπήλαιον λῃστῶν (vii. 11, cf. Mk. xi. 17, Lk. xix. 46). It will be destroyed, like the earlier temple at Shiloh, and Jerusalem and the other cities of Judah will be sacked, and the whole land laid waste—εἰς ἐρήμωσιν² ἔσται πᾶσα ἡ γῆ (vii. 34). Similarly in xxii. 5, εἰς ἐρήμωσιν ἔσται ὁ οἶκος οὗτος (viz. either the Temple or the royal palace). In chapter xxxii³ we have an impassioned proclamation of divine judgment upon the guilty nations, beginning with 'Jerusalem and the cities of Judah'—τοῦ θεῖναι αὐτὰς εἰς ἐρήμωσιν καὶ εἰς ἄβατον (xxxii. 4).

When the blow has fallen, and the Babylonian forces are in occupation of the devastated site of Jerusalem, the catastrophe is described retrospectively in similar terms. The prophet, now a refugee in Egypt, is represented as speaking to the Jewish colony there; because of the wickedness of the Jews (he says) the wrath of God blazed in the cities of Judah and the streets of Jerusalem, καὶ ἐγενήθησαν εἰς ἐρήμωσιν καὶ εἰς ἄβατον (li. 6); and again, ἐγενήθη ἡ γῆ ὑμῶν εἰς ἐρήμωσιν καὶ εἰς ἄβατον καὶ εἰς ἀρὰν ὡς ἐν τῇ ἡμέρᾳ ταύτῃ (*ibid.*, 22).

---

¹ Some MSS. differ.　　　² Codex Sinaiticus reads ἔρημον.

³ The reference here, as all through this article, is to Swete's text of the LXX. The Hebrew and English arrangement of chapters differs, sometimes substantially.

F

In view of all this, it is clear that if Luke (or the sponsors of his tradition) wished to speak of the fall of Jerusalem, whether in prospect or in retrospect, there is no word which would more naturally have suggested itself than ἐρήμωσις. It is hardly too much to say that for him and his readers ἐγένετο ἡ ἐρήμωσις αὐτῆς would mean: The final judgment upon Jerusalem, foreshadowed in prophecy and in the events of past history, has now fallen.

There appears therefore to be no sufficient reason for supposing that Lk. xxi. 20 is a mere 'editing' of Mark xiii. 14. On the contrary, it seems probable that Mk. xiii. 14-18, and Lk. xxi. 20-4 (or more exactly 20, 21b-22, 23b-24), represent diverse forms which an oracle upon the fate of Jerusalem and the Temple assumed in the pre-canonical tradition, though in the gospel as it stands the Lucan oracle has been supplemented out of Mark.

It is evident that this Lucan oracle has some affinity with the other passage about the fall of Jerusalem, xix. 42-4, although the latter does not show the rhythm and parallelism characteristic of Hebrew prophetic style. The description of military operations is here more detailed. The enemy is to construct a palisade, encircle the city so as to invest it completely, and finally raze it to the ground. This is in fact what happened, broadly speaking, in the war of A.D. 66-70. It is generally taken for granted that we have here a *vaticinium ex eventu*. But these operations are no more than the regular commonplaces of ancient warfare. In Josephus's account of the Roman capture of Jerusalem there are some features which are more distinctive; such as the fantastic faction-fighting which continued all through the siege, the horrors of pestilence and famine (including cannibalism), and finally the conflagration in which the Temple and a large part of the city perished. It is these that caught the imagination of Josephus, and, we may suppose, of any other witness of these events. Nothing is said of them here. On the other hand, among all the barbarities which Josephus reports, he does not say that the conquerors dashed children to the ground.[1] The expression ἐδαφιοῦσίν σε

[1] All the inhabitants under the age of 17 were sold into slavery: Josephus, *B.J.* vi. 418.

καὶ τὰ τέκνα σου ἐν σοί is in any case not based upon anything that happened in 66–70: it is a commonplace of Hebrew prophecy. Hosea, warning Israel of disasters to come, recalls the atrocities committed by a foreign invader in a recent campaign: μητέρα ἐπὶ τέκνοις ἠδάφισαν (x. 14); and goes on to threaten Samaria with a similar fate in a passage which may be quoted in full because it has several points of contact with the predictions in the gospels (Hos. xiv. 1):

ἀφανισθήσεται Σαμάρεια, ὅτι ἀντέστη πρὸς τὸν θεὸν αὐτῆς · ἐν ῥομφαίᾳ πεσοῦνται αὐτοί, καὶ τὰ ὑποτίτθια αὐτῶν ἐδαφισθήσονται, καὶ αἱ ἐν γαστρὶ ἔχουσαι αὐτῶν διαρραγήσονται (cf. Mk. xiii.17).

For the southern prophets, the fate of Samaria was in some sort a foreshadowing of the fate of Jerusalem. The spirit of revenge suggested a similar fate for the enemy, whether Assyria, the enemy of Samaria, or Babylon, the enemy of Jerusalem. Thus Nahum prophesies against Nineveh: αὐτὴ εἰς μετοικεσίαν πορεύσεται αἰχμάλωτος καὶ τὰ νήπια αὐτῆς ἐδαφιοῦσιν (iii. 10); and a Psalmist curses Babylon: μακάριος ὃς κρατήσει καὶ ἐδαφιεῖ τὰ νήπιά σου πρὸς τὴν πέτραν (Ps. cxxxvi. 9).[1] The same verb is sometimes used also of razing a city to the ground. Thus Isaiah prophesies against Jerusalem: οἱ ἰσχύοντες ὑμῶν μαχαίρᾳ πεσοῦνται καὶ ταπεινωθήσονται ... καὶ καταλειφθήσῃ μόνη καὶ εἰς τὴν γῆν ἐδαφισθήσῃ (iii. 25–6). The Lucan passage combines both senses of the verb in a single sentence.

The fact is that the whole significant vocabulary of both Lucan passages belongs to the language of the Septuagint, and is for the most part characteristic of the prophetical books; and what is still more to the point, several of these terms tend to recur alike in prophecies of the doom of Jerusalem and in historical accounts of its capture by Nebuchadrezzar in 586 B.C.

Take first the following terms referring to military operations: παρεμβάλλειν, χάραξ,[2] κυκλοῦν and περικυκλοῦν, συνέχειν

---

[1] In view of these passages, Wellhausen's suggestion that καὶ τὰ τέκνα σου ἐν σοί represents an Aramaic circumstantial clause, 'thy children being in thee' does not commend itself.

[2] χάραξ is properly a 'stake': Hellenistic writers use it collectively

('invest'), στρατόπεδον ('army'). All these are found as military terms in the Septuagint. There is nothing very remarkable about that; they are not unusual terms. But some of the combinations in which they occur are significant.

When the Assyrian forces were advancing on Judaea in the last years of the eighth century B.C., Isaiah at first expected an immediate siege and reduction of Jerusalem: κυκλώσω ὡς Δαυείδ[1] ἐπὶ σέ, καὶ βαλῶ περὶ σὲ χάρακα (xxix. 3). As the campaign developed, he became convinced that the city would escape after all: οὕτως λέγει Κύριος ἐπὶ βασιλέα ᾿Ασσυρίων, Οὐ μὴ εἰσέλθῃ εἰς τὴν πόλιν ταύτην, οὐδὲ μὴ βάλῃ ἐπ᾿ αὐτὴν βέλος . . . οὐδὲ μὴ κυκλώσῃ ἐπ᾿ αὐτὴν χάρακα (xxxvii. 33).

When again in the sixth century B.C., Jerusalem was threatened by Babylon, Ezekiel was instructed to warn his countrymen of their imminent danger by drawing a picture of the siege of a city on a tile and exhibiting it to them: λάβε σεαυτῷ πλίνθον . . . καὶ διαγράψεις ἐπ᾿ αὐτὴν πόλιν τὴν ῾Ιερουσαλήμ, καὶ δώσεις ἐπ᾿ αὐτὴν περιοχήν . . . καὶ περιβαλεῖς ἐπ᾿ αὐτὴν χάρακα, καὶ δώσεις ἐπ᾿ αὐτὴν παρεμβολάς, καὶ τάξεις τάς βελοστάσεις κύκλῳ . . . καὶ συγκλείσεις αὐτήν · σημεῖόν ἐστιν τοῦτο τοῖς υἱοῖς ᾿Ισραήλ (iv. 1–3). In a later prophecy, he pictures the King of Babylon as standing at the parting of the ways and using divination to decide whether he shall turn against Ammon or against Judah. In the issue, ἐγένετο τὸ μαντεῖον ἐπὶ ῾Ιερουσαλήμ . . . τοῦ βαλεῖν χάρακα ἐπὶ τὰς πύλας αὐτῆς, καὶ βαλεῖν χῶμα καὶ οἰκοδομῆσαι βελοστάσεις (xxi. 22).

The account of the eventual siege and capture of the city by Nebuchadrezzar has come down to us in the Septuagint in two slightly different forms. In Jer. lii. 4–5, we read, καὶ ἐγένετο τῷ ἔτει τῷ ἐνάτῳ τῆς βασιλείας αὐτοῦ . . . ἦλθεν Ναβουχοδονοσὸρ βασιλεὺς Βαβυλῶνος καὶ πᾶσα ἡ δύναμις αὐτοῦ ἐπὶ

---

for a 'palisade'. Josephus uses the more correct χαράκωμα (*B.J.* v. 269 etc.), as does Symmachus in his version of Jeremiah. The Septuagint always has χάραξ. The word does not occur in the NT outside this passage.

[1] i.e. presumably as David did when he captured the city from the Jebusites. The Massoretic text, however, has a different reading (דּוּר for דָּוִד).

Ἰερουσαλήμ, καὶ περιεχαράκωσαν αὐτὴν καὶ περιῳκοδόμησαν αὐτὴν τετραπόδοις κύκλῳ, καὶ ἦλθεν ἡ πόλις εἰς συνοχήν. (The verb συνέχειν does not occur in these contexts; it is used as a military term in I Kingdoms xxiii, 8, II Macc. ix, 2 ἐπεχείρηοεν ἱεροσυλεῖν καὶ τὴν πόλιν συνέχειν.) The parallel passage in IV Kingdoms xxv. 1–2 runs: . . . ἦλθεν N. βασιλεὺς B. καὶ πᾶσα ἡ δύναμις αὐτοῦ ἐπὶ Ἰερουσαλήμ, καὶ παρενέβαλεν ἐπ᾽ αὐτήν, καὶ ᾠκοδόμησεν ἐπ᾽ αὐτὴν περίτειχος κύκλῳ, καὶ ἦλθεν ἡ πόλις ἐν περιοχῇ.

There is a further reference to Nebuchadrezzar's attack in Jer. xli. 1, N. Βασιλεὺς B. καὶ πᾶν τὸ στρατόπεδον αὐτοῦ καὶ πᾶσα ἡ γῆ ἀρχῆς αὐτοῦ ἐπολέμουν ἐπὶ Ἰερουσαλήμ. It might seem idle to illustrate so common a term as στρατόπεδον, but it is a word strange to the Greek of the New Testament, with the sole exception of Lk. xxi. 20. In Acts xxiii. 27, Luke uses στράτευμα, which is also the word employed for a military force in Rev. ix. 16; xix. 14, 19.

For further illustration of some of these terms the following passages may be cited:

Jer. xxvii. 29 (Babylon is to suffer the fate she had inflicted on Jerusalem), παρεμβάλετε ἐπ᾽ αὐτὴν κυκλόθεν . . . ἀνταπόδοτε αὐτῇ κατὰ τὰ ἔργα αὐτῆς.

I Macc. xv. 13–14, παρενέβαλεν Ἀντίοχος ἐπὶ Δωρά . . . καὶ ἐκύκλωσεν τὴν πόλιν.

Ezek. xxvi. 8 (Babylonian attack on Tyre), ποιήσει ἐπί σε κύκλῳ χάρακα.

This accounts for all the military terms before us except περικυκλοῦν, which does not occur in contexts referring to the fall of Jerusalem; but cf. Jos. vii. 9, IV Kingdoms vi. 14 (Syrian siege of Dothan) ἀπέστειλεν ἐκεῖ ἵππον καὶ ἅρμα καὶ δύναμιν βαρεῖαν, καὶ ἦλθον νυκτὸς καὶ περιεκύκλωσαν τὴν πόλιν.

We might perhaps add to the military terms the verb ἐκχωρεῖν ('withdraw'), which is used as such in I Macc. ix. 62, ἐξεχώρησεν Ἰωναθὰν καὶ Σιμὼν καὶ οἱ μετ᾽ αὐτοῦ εἰς Βεθβασί. But in Numbers xvi. 45, the verb is used of the secession of Moses and Aaron from a rebellious people, about to suffer punishment for their sins: ἐκχωρήσατε ἐκ μέσου τῆς συναγωγῆς ταύτης καὶ ἐξαναλώσω αὐτοὺς εἰς ἅπαξ. This is perhaps nearer to the sense in Lk. xxi. 21: Christians are to secede in time from the doomed community.

The remaining terms may be illustrated more briefly.

Καιρός ἐπισκοπῆς, Jer. vi. 15 (oracle on the Enemy from the North, see above), x. 15. *Ἐπισκοπή* in the sense of a divine 'visitation', whether favourable or unfavourable, *passim*.

Ἡμέραι ἐκδικήσεως, Hos. ix. 7 (the doom of Israel), ἥκασιν αἱ ἡμέραι τῆς ἐκδικήσεως, Jer. xxvi. 10, ἡ ἡμέρα ἐκείνη Κυρίῳ τῷ θεῷ ἡμῶν ἡμέρα ἐκδικήσεως τοῦ ἐκδικῆσαι τοὺς ἐχθροὺς αὐτοῦ. Cf. Jer. xxvi. 21, xxvii, 27, 31 (note παρεμβάλετε ἐπ' αὐτὴν κυκλόθεν in the immediate context), etc.

Ἀνάγκη μεγάλη, Zeph. i. 14–15 (a *locus classicus* of prophetic eschatology), ἐγγὺς ἡμέρα Κυρίου ἡ μεγάλη . . . ἡμέρα ὀργῆς ἡ ἡμέρα ἐκείνη, ἡμέρα θλίψεως καὶ ἀνάγκης.

Ὀργὴ τῷ λαῷ τούτῳ. The conception of the ὀργὴ Κυρίου (θεοῦ), is ubiquitous in the Old Testament, but note the impersonal ὀργή ('retribution'), as here, II Chron. xxiv. 18, ἐγένετο ὀργὴ ἐπὶ Ἰουδὰ καὶ Ἰερουσαλήμ, Ps. lxxvii. 21, πῦρ ἀνήφθη ἐν Ἰακώβ, καὶ ὀργὴ ἀνέβη ἐπὶ τὸν Ἰσραήλ, etc. Cf. also Zephaniah *l.c. supra*.

Πεσοῦνται στόματι μαχαίρης, Jer. xx. 4–6 (forecast of the Babylonian conquest) πεσοῦνται ἐν μαχαίρᾳ ἐχθρῶν αὐτῶν . . . καὶ σὺ καὶ πάντες οἱ κατοικοῦντες ἐν τῷ οἴκῳ σου πορεύσεσθε ἐν αἰχμαλωσίᾳ, Id. xxi. 7 (the same) κατακόψουσιν αὐτοὺς ἐν στόματι μαχαίρας. Cf. Jer. xvi. 4, II Kingdoms xv. 14, etc.

Αἰχμαλωτισθήσονται εἰς πάντα τὰ ἔθνη. Amos v. 5, Γάλγαλα (the ancient Israelite sanctuary) αἰχμαλωτευομένη αἰχμαλωτευθήσεται. From Amos on, this becomes a regular theme of prophecy. Cf. also Tobit i. 10, ὅτε ἠχμαλωτίσθημεν εἰς Νινευή, Deut. xxviii. 64, διασπερεῖ σε Κύριος ὁ θεός σου εἰς πάντα τὰ ἔθνη.

Ἱερουσαλὴμ ἔσται πατουμένη ὑπὸ ἐθνῶν. Zech. xii. 3, θήσομαι τὴν Ἱερουσαλὴμ λίθον καταπατούμενον πᾶσι τοῖς ἔθνεσιν.

Ἄχρι οὗ πληρωθῶσιν καιροὶ ἐθνῶν. The precise phrase does not occur, but the idea is present: Daniel vii. 25 (of the last heathen king) παραδοθήσεται πάντα εἰς τὰς χεῖρας αὐτοῦ ἕως καιροῦ καὶ καιρῶν καὶ ἕως ἡμίσους καιροῦ. Ib. ix. 26–7, Βασι-

λεία ἐθνῶν φθερεῖ τὴν πόλιν καὶ τὸ ἅγιον . . . κατὰ συντέλειαν
καιρῶν . . . ἕως καιροῦ συντελείας πολέμου, καὶ ἀφαιρεθήσεται
ἡ ἐρήμωσις.[1]

It appears, then, that not only are the two Lucan oracles composed *entirely* from the language of the Old Testament, but the conception of the coming disaster which the author has in mind is a generalized picture of the fall of Jerusalem as imaginatively presented by the prophets. So far as any historical event has coloured the picture, it is not Titus's capture of Jerusalem in A.D. 70, but Nebuchadrezzar's capture in 586 B.C. There is no single trait of the forecast which cannot be documented directly out of the Old Testament.

Not only is the vocabulary biblical; the idiom is markedly Semitic at several points. This creates a certain presumption that the evangelist is not here composing freely, since he elsewhere shows himself capable of writing pure Hellenistic Greek. Some critics, indeed, believe that Luke sometimes wrote, deliberately, a *pastiche* of Septuagintal Greek. The question would need to be discussed upon a broader basis than these two passages. But there is here a special reason for supposing that at least in xxi. 20-4 he is making use of older material: the Marcan language of 21*a*, 23*a*, stands out like a patch upon an otherwise homogeneous fabric, which must therefore have existed before our present Third Gospel was composed.

There seems then to be a high probability that the evangelist is dependent upon previously existing sources, whether oral or written. We may describe them as oracles in the manner of the ancient prophets, which circulated in Judaea before Titus's siege of Jerusalem, but at a time when a war with Rome was a menacing possibility—as it must have seemed to far-seeing minds at any date after the rebellion of Judas the Gaulonite in

[1] To a Christian reader—at least to one acquainted with Paul's theology—the 'fulfilment of the times of the Gentiles' might suggest the progress of Gentile Christianity (cf. Rom. xi. 25-6). But no such idea has influenced Luke's text, where we have, without any modification, the prophetic conception of Gentile oppression of the Holy City in retribution for its sins.

A.D. 6. Whether these oracles were Jewish or Christian in origin, the evidence of these passages themselves does not permit us to say with certainty. In Christian circles they were believed to go back to Jesus.

Finally, we return briefly to Mk. xiii. 14–20, which we shall now regard, not as a source which Luke has 'edited', but as an alternative form of oracle upon the approaching disasters in Judaea. As I have already remarked, the Marcan passage is less homogeneous than the two Lucan oracles. It is by no means clear that it offers a consistent picture of forthcoming events.

Verses 17–18 are naturally, and no doubt rightly, understood as referring to the sufferings of the civil population in a country overrun by the enemy (for 17, cf. Hosea xiv. 1, cited above, also Amos i. 3, 13; IV Kingdoms viii. 12; xv. 16). Verses 15–16, in this context, refer to the necessity of *instant* flight when the quick-marching Roman armies are advancing. In Lk. xvii. 31, the same saying, with slight verbal variations, occurs in a different context, enforced by an allusion to the fate of Lot's wife, who failed to make her escape when Sodom was destroyed by fire from heaven. The destruction of Sodom, and Noah's deluge, are here treated as prototypes of the final catastrophe, the 'Day of the Son of Man', delineated in the spirit of Amos's prophecy of the 'Day of the Lord', which is, 'darkness and not light' (Amos v. 18). It must, however, be admitted that the reference to flight in time of war seems more appropriate, since even instant flight, as indeed Amos himself indicates (v. 19), would be of little avail in the ultimate catastrophe, which covers the earth like a single lightning-flash from end to end of the sky (Lk. xvii. 24). Mark, however, has added in verses 19–20 a comment which seems to identify the situation described in 15–18 with the final 'tribulation', threatening the destruction of the entire human race, and so to bring it all back into an 'apocalyptic' setting, similar to that of Lk. xvii.

This description of coming calamities is introduced in Mk. xiii. 14 by a cryptic allusion to the βδέλυγμα ἐρημώσεως. The reference (as Matthew has indicated in an editorial note, xxvi. 15) is to passages in 'Daniel the prophet': xi. 31; xii. 11). There it signifies the idolatrous image which Antiochus

Epiphanes set up in the Temple at Jerusalem in 168–167 B.C.: Ζεὺς Οὐράνιος ('Ολύμπιος), in Hebrew בעל שמים, which, by a kind of opprobrious paraphrase not unfamiliar in the Old Testament, becomes שקוץ שמם, 'the abominable thing (i.e. idol) which devastates', or 'which appals', the verb שמם (suggested by the consonants of שמים) having both meanings. The Septuagint translators have chosen the former meaning and rendered it by βδέλυγμα ἐρημώσεως, which as Greek is meaningless, but serves no less well for that as an apocalyptic cryptogram. The expression recurs in I Macc. i. 54, with reference to the same episode, and nowhere else until it reappears in Mark. It must point, here also, to an idolatrous profanation of the Temple.[1] Mark has strangely construed a masculine participle, ἑστηκότα, with the neuter βδέλυγμα, as though he intended the cryptogram to be read back into a personal name, not perhaps Ζεὺς Οὐράνιος, but the name of some heathen deity or other whose image is to be set up for worship—possibly the divine emperor, if we adopt the conjecture (originally offered, I believe, by B. W. Bacon and widely accepted) that interest in Daniel's prophecy was revived by the attempt of the Emperor Gaius to introduce his image into the Temple, A.D. 40. (Josephus, *Antiquities*, xviii. 261–309. The horror and alarm which the proposal aroused among the Jews is reflected in the indignant rhetoric of Philo's *Legatio ad Gaium*.) It may well be that the whole episode recalled to mind the sacrilege of Antiochus Epiphanes—and the revolt which followed. In I Macc ii. we are told how, after the βδέλυγμα ἐρημώσεως had been erected in Jerusalem, the priest Mattathias made his protest by killing a Jew who approached the pagan altar at his own town of Modein, and then took to the hills with his sons—ἔφυγον αὐτὸς καὶ οἱ υἱοὶ αὐτοῦ εἰς τὰ ὄρη (ii. 28)—and were there joined by numbers of Jewish patriots who formed the nucleus of a 'national resistance movement'.

[1] It is difficult indeed to see how, with its well-established associations, the expression could suggest to any instructed 'editor' the idea of 'Jerusalem encircled by armies'. Luke was probably not a Jew, but he knew his Septuagint too well to fall into such an error. He preferred his own source.

The words of Mk. xiii. 15, οἱ ἐν τῇ ᾿Ιουδαίᾳ φευγέτωσαν εἰς τὰ ὄρη, seem reminiscent of the language of I Macc. ii. 28; and as Mattathias and his sons left their property behind them —ἐνκατέλειπον ὅσα εἶχον ἐν τῇ πόλει—the injunction in xiii. 15–16 would fit a similar situation, although, as we have seen, its original context is uncertain.

Whereas, therefore, in the Lucan oracles the prototype of coming disaster is the Babylonian capture of Jerusalem in 586 B.C., in Mark its prototype is the sacrilege of Antiochus in 168–7 B.C. A new Antiochus will commit a new sacrilege, and those to whom the oracle was originally addressed are to be the new Maccabees. Whether these were Jews or Christians (more properly, Christian or non-Christian Jews) is a question more easily asked than answered.[1]

It does not, however, appear that there is an original or necessary connection between Mk. xiii. 14, and the composite passage which it now introduces. Verses 15–18 would fit readily into the framework of a general forecast of the devastation, or ἐρήμωσις, of Jerusalem. Indeed, if Mark (or his immediate authority) worked upon a tradition which used the term ἐρήμωσις in the sense which is so common in Old Testament prophecy, he might well have been led on to think of the βδέλυγμα ἐρημώσεως of Daniel, especially under the stimulus, it may be, of Gaius's attempted sacrilege. In any case it seems as if he were aware of introducing into a familiar context an unfamiliar idea, which calls for some 'searching of

[1] It is widely held that the Marcan oracle of the βδέλυγμα ἐρημώσεως is closely related to the prediction of the ἄνθρωπος τῆς ἀνομίας in II Thess. ii 3–10. Some connection there may be, but it is hazardous to identify the two figures, or to find in II Thess. a key to the 'apocalypse' of Mk. xiii. The ἄνθρωπος τῆς ἀνομίας is an 'antichrist' figure, combining traits of Beliar in the *Testament of Dan* with those of 'Lucifer' in Is. xiv. 12–14—to go no further into his manifold antecedents. It is not clear that the βδέλυγμα ἐρημώσεως is properly an 'antichrist' at all. If so, he comes on the scene too early, for the only proper setting for 'antichrist' in the Marcan sequence of events (so far as it conforms to apocalyptic tradition) is at xiii. 22, where his place seems to be taken by a plurality of 'pseudochrists'.

the Scriptures': hence the curious note, ὁ ἀναγινώσκων νοείτω. If so, then it is Mark, and not Luke, which is 'secondary'.

This, however, is speculative. We seem in any case to be led to the conclusion that of the alternative forms of oracle the Lucan is consistent and readily intelligible from well-known passages of the Old Testament, while the Marcan shows signs of composition from dispersed material and remains obscure. How far either or both may be regarded as representing with substantial truth some aspects of the teaching of Jesus is a question which needs a wider basis for discussion than these brief *pericopae*.

7 The Historical Problem of the Death of Jesus

The death of Jesus Christ is a fact lying near the heart of our Christian faith. It is also an episode in the history of the Roman province of Judaea during the half-century before the Jewish War. As such, it presents a problem of its own, apart from the question of its theological interpretation, and it is this problem that I propose to ventilate here.

The historian Tacitus, reporting the measures taken by Nero against the Christians in Rome, informs his readers that 'Christ, from whom the name is derived, was executed in the reign of Tiberius by the procurator Pontius Pilate. The pestilent superstition,' he adds, 'though repressed for the moment, broke out afresh, not only in Judaea, where the mischief began, but also in Rome, where everything vile and horrible finds its way.'[1] According to this writer, therefore (expressing, we may suppose, the official government view), Jesus was put to death by sentence of a Roman magistrate for promulgating religious teachings intolerable in a civilized society.

The Jewish account of the matter is different. The tractate *Sanhedrin* in the Babylonian Talmud contains the following statement: 'Jesus was hanged on the Eve of Passover. The herald went before him for forty days, saying: "He is going forth to be stoned because he practised sorcery (כִּישֵׁף) and enticed (הֵיסִית) and led astray (הִדִּיחַ) Israel. Let everyone knowing anything in his defence come and plead for him." But nothing was found in his defence, so he was hanged on the Eve of Passover.'[2] The two verbs rendered 'enticed' and 'led astray' (hiphils of סות, נדח respectively) are the same two used in the law of Deut. xiii. 1–11, which I quote, abridging the legal verbiage: 'When a prophet or dreamer appears among you . . . and calls on you to follow other gods . . . that prophet or dreamer shall be put to death, for he has preached rebellion

---

[1] Tacitus, *Annals*, XV. 44.   [2] *Bab. Sanh.* 43.

against the Lord your God; he has tried to *lead you astray* (לְהַדִּיחֲךָ).... If your brother or ... your dearest friend should *entice* (יְסִיתְךָ) you secretly to go and worship other gods ... you shall have no pity on him ... you shall stone him to death, because he tried to *lead you astray* (לְהַדִּיחֲךָ).' It is clear, therefore, that the passage in *Sanhedrin* is intended to show that Jesus was condemned and put to death under the provisions of the Jewish law for the crime of attempting to lead Jewish people into apostasy from their religion. The reference to sorcery may also have a side-glance at the law of Deut. xiii, for it is there contemplated that the false prophet may perform a sign or a wonder to back up his pernicious doctrines. The punishment assigned for the crime of 'enticing' and 'leading astray' is stoning. The tractate does not state that Jesus was stoned; it says that he was condemned to stoning, and was hanged. The verb תלה, תלא is used of the gibbeting of the bodies of executed criminals: 'When a man is convicted of a capital crime and put to death, you shall hang him on a gibbet (תָלִיתָ אֹתוֹ עַל־עֵץ)' (Deut. xxi. 22); and specifically, 'All who have been stoned must be hanged' (*Mishna Sanhedrin* 6. 4). On this showing, therefore, Jesus was rightly condemned and executed, entirely within the framework of Jewish law and practice, and obviously by Jewish authorities, for promulgating false and pernicious teachings. It is true that Babylonian *Sanhedrin* is a relatively late tractate, and some critics discount its evidence on that score; but it is certain that even late tractates often contain traditional material which may be of quite early derivation. The passage could not derive from Christian sources, and it may be taken as evidence for a Jewish view of the death of Jesus possessing at any rate respectable talmudic authority.

To these two extraneous witnesses we may add a third, perhaps of more dubious value. A Stoic philosopher of the name of Mara bar Sarapion, of Samosata, is the author of an epistle[1] in which, among other topics, he speaks of the persecution of the wise and virtuous, and its ultimate futility.

---

[1] *Epistle of Mara, son of Sarapion*, in Cureton, *Spicilegium Syriacum*: Syriac text, pp. 43–8, translation, pp. 70–6.

He adduces the examples of Pythagoras, Socrates, and a wise king of the Jews. 'What advantage', he asks, 'did the Jews gain by the death of their wise king, seeing that from that same time their kingdom was taken away? . . . Socrates is not dead, because of Plato, nor Pythagoras, because of the statue of Hera, nor the wise king, because of the new laws he gave.' The wise king of the Jews can hardly be meant for anyone but Jesus, though Mara's ideas about him are a bit confused (hardly more so, indeed, than about Pythagoras).[1] Late though the epistle is—probably as late as the third century—it may well represent the way in which a somewhat vague memory of the death of Jesus filtered through in some thoughtful circles in the pagan world. It could not be derived from Jewish sources, and a Christian source is hardly more likely. It goes beyond the sources already cited in stating that Jesus died as 'king of the Jews'. But basically the description of him as a wise king who gave new laws, especially in a work by a Stoic philosopher (for whom it is an axiom that the wise man is the only true king), is not different from the conception of him as an influential teacher which we have found in our other sources. The parallel with Socrates, who was put to death by the Athenians because they thought his teaching pernicious in its influence, clearly suggests that Jesus was put to death by his countrymen for a similar reason.

These three extraneous witnesses, then, agree that Jesus suffered a violent death as the promulgator of unacceptable teaching, while differing with regard to the authority by which the penalty was inflicted.

I now turn to Christian sources, and first to two passages in the Acts of the Apostles. Acts x. 39 refers to 'Jesus of Nazareth whom they put to death by hanging on a gibbet'. The Greek phrase, κρεμάσαι ἐπὶ ξύλου, is the LXX translation of the תָּלָה עַל־עֵץ of Deuteronomy. The subject of the verb is here left undefined; the indefinite third plural represents the Aramaic idiom for the passive. (The same idiom is found in the Hebrew of *Bab. Sanh.* 43.) But in Acts v. 30 Peter, addres-

---

[1] The philosopher Pythagoras is confused with a sculptor of the same name.

sing 'the High Priest and those who were with him', says, '*You* put him to death by hanging on a gibbet', ὃν ὑμεῖς διεχειρίσασθε κρεμάσαντες ἐπὶ ξύλου. This tallies closely with the statement in *Bab. Sanh.* There is one other occurrence of the expression κρεμάσαι ἐπὶ ξύλου, in Gal. iii. 13, where Paul quotes from Deut. xxi. 23, 'Cursed is everyone who is hanged on a gibbet', ἐπικατάρατος πᾶς ὁ κρεμάμενος ἐπὶ ξύλου. This is the LXX translation of קִלְלַת אֱלֹהִים תָּלוּי, which is the conclusion of the Deuteronomic law (already quoted) about the gibbeting of the bodies of criminals. The inference I should draw is that the manner in which Jesus was put to death was accepted as the equivalent of the stoning and gibbeting which was the penalty prescribed in the Torah for the crime of 'enticing' and 'leading astray', and that the responsibility for it was attributed, both by Christians and in the Jewish tradition represented by *Bab. Sanh.*, to the Jewish authorities.

In other passages of the N.T. the verb used is not κρεμάσαι but σταυροῦν, 'crucify'. Crucifixion was not a punishment recognized in Jewish law or practice, but it was widely employed by the Romans throughout their provincial empire. In the epistles the verb is almost invariably in the passive, and the agent is not indicated.[1]

In two passages of Acts, however, ii. 36 and iv. 10, Peter, addressing Jewish audiences, refers to 'Jesus whom *you* crucified', ὃν ὑμεῖς ἐσταυρώσατε. It is impossible that this should be true, taken *au pied de la lettre*. It must be understood in the light of another passage, Acts ii. 23, where Peter, choosing his words with more care, says 'You killed him by fastening him (to a cross) through the agency of heathen men', τοῦτον ... διὰ χειρὸς ἀνόμων προσπήξαντες ἀνείλατε. That is to say, Jesus died by the Roman method of crucifixion, but the Romans were carrying out the intention of the Jewish authorities, and *qui facit per alium facit per se*. In Acts iv. 26 a certain collaboration between Jews and Romans is suggested: 'Herod

---

[1] The only exception, in passages when Jesus is the object of the verb, is I Cor. ii. 8, where the agents are said to be the ἄρχοντες τοῦ αἰῶνος τούτου, i.e. the superhuman powers believed to have some control over events in the sublunary sphere.

and Pontius Pilate conspired with the Gentiles and the people of Israel.' The language here is adapted to that of Psalm ii, 1–2, which is cited as a *testimonium*,[1] but that is not necessarily to say that the statement is nothing more than a reflection of the prophecy.

So much, then, we may learn from the writings of the N.T. outside the gospels. It provides a background against which we should place the gospel narratives. To these I now turn.

The gospels purport to give a somewhat detailed account of the trial and execution of Jesus, and the events that preceded. They differ in some details, but the general sequence is common to all four. All agree that Jesus was crucified. The punishment of stoning, mentioned in the Jewish tradition, has no place in the gospel account. It is, however, perhaps not altogether without significance that the Fourth Gospel reports an abortive attempt at stoning, some time before the finally successful attack at the Passover season (John viii. 59). Is it possible that behind both the Fourth Gospel and *Bab. Sanh.* lies a somewhat dim memory that in the eyes of Jewish authorities Jesus was *liable* to the penalty of stoning, as prescribed in the Mosaic Law, even though it may not in fact have been inflicted (which, as we have seen, is the view implied in *Bab. Sanh.*)? In any case, the gospels know only of the Roman penalty of crucifixion, and in harmony with this all four agree that it was inflicted by sentence of a Roman court. The judge is the prefect[2] Pontius Pilate, the accusers—playing the part, in our way of speaking, of both counsel and witnesses for the prosecution—are the Jewish leaders, variously described as 'chief priests' (Mark), 'chief priests and elders' (Matt.), the Sanhedrin as a body (Luke), or vaguely 'the Jews' (John). It is in this capacity, and in no other, that they figure in the report. On this point there is no difference among our sources. The whole process—accusation, hearing, examination, verdict, sentence—is carried through in the prefect's court,

---

[1] See C. H. Dodd, *According to the Scriptures* (Nisbet, 1952), p. 105, *Historical Tradition in the Fourth Gospel*, pp. 117–18.

[2] *Præfectus* not *procurator*, in spite of Tacitus. See *Historical Tradition in the Fourth Gospel*, p. 96.

and the convicted Prisoner is put to death in the Roman
fashion.

But what was the charge, and what the crime of which the
Prisoner was convicted? On this point our sources are less
informative. Mark and Matthew say no more than that the
priests brought 'many' charges. In John, to Pilate's formal
question, 'What charge do you bring?' the accusers answer
vaguely that the Prisoner is a 'wrongdoer' (κακὸν ποιῶν).
Luke is a little more precise. He draws up a charge sheet, with
colourable similarity to known Roman forms. There are three
counts: (i) 'subverting the nation', (ii) opposing the payment
of taxes to the Emperor, (iii) claiming to be a king. When
Pilate reports that he finds the Prisoner not guilty on these
counts, the prosecution insists, 'His teaching is causing dis-
affection among the people'. The terms used, διαστρέφοντα
τὸ ἔθνος, ἀνασείει τὸν λαόν, are curiously reminiscent of the
language of *Bab. Sanh.*, according to which Jesus was convicted of 'enticing' and 'leading astray' Israel.[1] If, however,
there is a real reminiscence underlying Luke's version of the
first count in the charge, he must have misunderstood the
'subversion' in a political sense; otherwise it would have no
interest for the Roman. The second count, that of opposing
the payment of taxes, could no doubt have been alleged; it
was the kind of charge to catch the ear of a Roman governor
who was on the watch for any possible imitator of Judas the
Gaulonite, whose revolt was raised precisely on this issue. But
we hear nothing further of this charge. Whatever other charges
there may have been, all the gospels represent Pilate as con-
centrating on what in Luke is the third count: the claim to
kingship. In all of them the crucial question addressed to the
Defendant is, 'Are you the king of the Jews?' In all of them
the reply is, Σὺ λέγεις. I can find no evidence that either in
Greek or in Aramaic this meant 'Yes'. It would appear to be
intentionally non-committal, meaning something like, 'The

---

[1] Ἀποστρέφειν and ἐπισείειν both appear in the LXX as trans-
lations of הֵסִית (entice). It is perhaps worth noting that in one place
(Ezek. xxxiv. 16) נדח is rendered by πλανᾶν, so that πλανᾷ τὸν ὄχλον
(Jn. vii. 12) would be a possible translation of הַדִּיחַ אֶת־יִשְׂרָאֵל.

G

words are yours', 'Have it so if you choose'.[1] On this basis, according to the Synoptics, Pilate pronounced sentence of death, taking the view, perhaps, that if the Prisoner does not deny the claim it is tantamount to an admission. And it was a fatal admission, for, as the accusers insist (in John), there could be only one βασιλεύς in the Roman empire, Tiberius.

John however does not leave it at that. His report of the examination *in camera* (xviii. 33–8) cannot, of course, be taken as anything like a transcript of the proceedings. The language has a strongly Johannine cast. But it would be unwise to leave it entirely out of account. It is at any rate the work of a writer who shows understanding of the situation in Roman Judaea in the years before the great revolt. What he says amounts to this: Jesus was not, as Pilate was intended to think, a resistance leader—obviously, since he had no followers under arms. A king he was, but not in a political sense. His mission was to 'testify to the truth'; his subjects were those who yield themselves to the truth. In other words, although the charge on which he was condemned was ostensibly political, in fact the point at issue was the character, and the effect, of his teaching. In this sense he was, as the Stoic writer says, a king who gave new laws. We may reasonably accept from John the hint that this issue did lie significantly in the background, and the matter is thus brought back into the perspective in which it was seen by our three extraneous witnesses. But directly, the death of Jesus was brought about by the action of the Roman administration of Judaea on the ground of constructive treason to the Empire.

The provincial administration had occasion to deal with several such rebel leaders, would-be kings of the Jews, in the half-century preceding the great revolt. The peculiarity of the case which Pilate had to try is that this alleged nationalist Pretender was arraigned, surprisingly, by the Jewish leaders themselves. On this all the gospel accounts agree, and only a radical scepticism which makes any historical criticism nugatory attempts to deny it. It is this that we have to try to

---

[1] Cf. *Apostolic Constitutions*, V. 14. 4: οὐκ εἶπεν ὁ Κύριος ὅτι 'ναί' ἀλλ' ὅτι 'σὺ εἶπας' (commenting on Matt. xxvi. 25).

understand. The prosecution was to all appearance a corporate and official action, in which the whole Sanhedrin was involved, though in all our sources we have the impression that the 'chief priests' are the really active participants. We should naturally presume that in order to organize the prosecution some preliminary investigation would take place. And in fact all gospels allow for something of the kind. In John we have the account of a meeting of 'chief priests and Pharisees' at which it was resolved that Jesus must be put to death, on the ground that his growing influence was only too likely to provoke Roman intervention on a disastrous scale (Jn. xi. 47–53). There is no confirmation of this in the other gospels, but the whole account in John is so much in agreement with what we know of Jewish attitudes and Jewish sentiment at the time that it may well be based on good information. This was before Jesus was arrested. After his arrest, according to John, he was brought before Annas, who questioned him 'about his teaching and about his disciples' (xviii. 19). If he was being arraigned, as the Talmud tells us, for misleading the people by false teaching, such interrogation would be quite pertinent, and once again it fits in with the evidence of our extraneous witnesses. But it does not help us to understand the framing of the charge before Pilate.

The Synoptics give an account of a meeting of the full Sanhedrin, at which charges were brought forward and witnesses heard (Matt. xxvi. 59–66, Mk. xiv. 55–64, Lk. xxii. 66–71). The three accounts are not wholly in agreement, but they all agree that the council convinced itself that Jesus was putting forward a claim to be 'Messiah', and this, though it was at that period a somewhat fluid term, connoted in the popular mind the expected national liberator and ruler, and it could easily be paraphrased for Roman ears as 'king of the Jews'.

The Synoptists evidently intend to depict a regular session of the Sanhedrin conducting a formal trial which ends (in Matthew and Mark, though not in Luke) with a vote of condemnation. Yet in spite of this the Sanhedrists appear before Pilate, not as judges seeking a confirmation of their verdict, but, unambiguously, as accusers. The apparent contradiction can be explained. The Sanhedrin was in the eyes of its own members the sovereign governing body of the people of Israel, with exclusive authority to interpret and enforce the divinely given law of Moses. In hard fact it was no more than a local organ of municipal administration, exercising just so much power as Rome chose to allow, and no more. This power certainly had a fairly wide range, for the imperial policy was liberal in its attitude to provincial institutions. Whether it extended to the infliction of the death penalty has been, and is, the subject of much controversy. John expressly asserts that it did not (xviii. 31), with some possible support from a *baraita* in the Palestinian Talmud.[1] From the standpoint of Roman law and practice it seems to me incredible that in Judaea under Roman rule the municipal authorities could have been allowed so exceptional a privilege.[2]

It would seem a reasonable reading of the evidence to say that the Jewish authorities—which means primarily the priesthood—had come to the conclusion that the growing influence of Jesus over the people was a menace to the security of the Jewish state and religion, and that he must be got out of the way. They could not themselves lawfully put him to death. A charge must therefore be formulated on which he might be arraigned before the prefect with fair certainty of a capital sentence. The proceedings which the Synoptics describe were

---

[1] Cited by S-B. (*ad* Mt. xxvii.2) from *Sanh.* i. 18a. 37, 7; 24b. 43.

[2] So far as we know it was confined to a few *civitates liberae*, a category to which Jerusalem did not belong. I am aware that there is weighty opinion on the other side. But see the most recent discussion from the Roman historian's point of view in A. N. Sherwin-White, *Roman Law and Society in the New Testament* (Oxford, 1963). Among the few recorded, or alleged, exceptions, the deaths of Stephen (Acts vi–vii) and of James, bishop of Jerusalem (Josephus, *Antiq.*, xx. 200), have the appearance of lynchings rather than legal executions, and the latter certainly, the former possibly, took place between the end of one governor's term of office and the arrival of his successor. No doubt on occasion a complaisant or politic governor might look the other way, but in the present case (if the view I have taken of it has any validity) it was important to Caiaphas that the proceedings should be above board and constitutional.

in Jewish eyes a regular trial under Mosaic law, ending in a formal condemnation, but in effect they were something more analogous to Grand Jury proceedings, determining the charge to be preferred before the competent court. The charge was, in Jewish terms, claiming to be Messiah; in terms fitted for Roman ears, claiming to be King of the Jews.

So far, so good. But Matthew and Mark (though not Luke) say that the actual crime of which Jesus was convicted by the Sanhedrin was that of 'blasphemy'. How such crime was related to the messianic claim is far from clear. We do not know what Hebrew terms the words βλασφημεῖν, βλασφημία, are here intended to represent, nor, consequently, which of the legal definitions or directions, whether in the Old Testament or in the Talmud, are supposed to have been applied in this case. The words are so excessively rare in the LXX (in books where a Hebrew original is extant) that we cannot expect much guidance from that source.[1] To attempt, therefore, to determine the meaning of a condemnation for 'blasphemy' through a minute examination of the language of this passage would seem an unprofitable enterprise. Since what we have is hardly more (in any case) than a *précis* by the evangelists, in their own

---

[1] βλασφημεῖν in fact occurs in five places only, representing 4 different expressions, 3 Hebrew and 1 Aramaic, and none of these have any obvious application to points brought out in the trial.

גִּדֵּף ('revile') IV Kms. xix. 6. τῶν λογίων ὧν ἐβλασφήμησαν
= הַדְּבָרִים אֲשֶׁר גִּדְּפוּ

IV Kms. xix. 22. ὠνείδισας καὶ ἐβλασφήμησας
= חֵרַפְתָּ וְגִדַּפְתָּ

יָכַח ('reprove') IV Kms. xix. 4. ὀνειδίζειν θεὸν ζῶντα καὶ
βλασφημεῖν. = לְחָרֵף אֱלֹהִים חַי וְהוֹכִיחַ

נָאַץ ('contemn') Isa. lii. 5. τὸ ὄνομά μου βλασφημεῖται
= שְׁמִי מִנֹּאָץ

אֲמַר שָׁלָה (= 'speak amiss'—but the text is uncertain)

Dan. iii. 96 (29) LXX, ὃς ἂν βλασφημήσῃ εἰς τὸν κύριον, Θ, ἐὰν
εἴπῃ βλασφημίας κατὰ τοῦ θεοῦ = דִּי יֵאמַר שָׁלָה עַל־אֱלָהֲהוֹן

[In Is. lxvi. 3 βλάσφημος seems to be a loose paraphrase of a misunderstood original.]

Greek, of proceedings which must have been conducted in Hebrew, it might be more useful to consider the sense in which the evangelists themselves use the terms βλασφημεῖν, βλασφημία, in other contexts.

I shall come to this presently, but for the moment I propose to approach the matter by a somewhat more circuitous route, starting from the hint contained in several of our sources— Christian, Jewish and pagan—that the hostility which brought about the death of Jesus was due to the character of his teaching, or, more properly, to fear of its effect on society. I ask, therefore, what there was in his teaching that gave offence. That he occupied a large measure of common ground with contemporary rabbis has been sufficiently shown in a number of recent studies. This is recognized by the evangelists themselves, if perhaps less amply than the true position might have justified. But in spite of it, they represent Jesus as being frequently in conflict with the custodians of Jewish orthodoxy, the 'scribes', and particularly those of the Pharisaic school. Some critics have maintained that all this is no more than a backlash from the bitter feelings which later arose between Church and Synagogue, and that Jesus himself could have had no quarrel with Pharisaism. It is likely enough that the antagonism has sometimes been sharpened in retrospect, but I do not believe that any legitimate criticism can disintegrate the general picture of conflict, or shake the evidence that the Pharisees were in a special degree a party to the conflict.

Let us recall a few of the points at which Jesus is reported to have been in conflict with the official representatives of Judaism—or of the school of Judaism predominant at the time. The recall can be very brief, since the ground is well trodden.

Jesus was censured for setting loose to the regulations for the Sabbath. He was accused of neglecting the rules for ceremonial purity, and retorted both with a cutting remark about the outside of the cup and platter and with the challenging utterance, 'Nothing that goes into a man from outside can defile him' (Mk. vii. 18).[1] It is pertinent to remember that the

---

[1] It is probable that we should find independent attestation of this saying in Rom. xiv. 14. See above, p. 25.

keeping of the Sabbath and scruples about kinds of food were two of the most distinctive marks of the Jewish way of life, as seen by outside observers. Not only so; heroes of the nation had given their lives in loyalty to the Sabbath and in obedience to the food laws. What martyrs have consecrated with their blood cannot be lightly regarded.

It was not that Jesus set out to undermine the religious practices or conventions of his people. His comment on the payment of tithe (Matt. xxiii. 23, Lk. xi. 42) indicates his general attitude: no harm in being strict about tithe, but justice, mercy and good faith are the weightier matters of the law and 'it is these you ought to have practised, without neglecting the others'. Tolerant and reasonable enough. But if you start making fine distinctions among the rules by which the divine law is safeguarded—some important, some unimportant—where will it end? So the Pharisees must have asked themselves. One can see their point. But Jesus said that in fact the traditional rules, instead of being a safeguard, had sometimes come to have the effect of 'making God's word null and void' (Mk. vii. 13)—which amounted to a frontal attack on the whole Pharisaic position. Again, he laid immense emphasis on the inwardness of true morality. Not that he undervalued the overt act—'*doing* the will of God'—but he refused to reckon as moral action anything that was not a true expression of a man's character, of the whole man: 'either make the tree good and the fruit good, or make the tree bad and the fruit bad' (Matt. xii. 33). There are few themes more pervasive in the Sayings. No Pharisee, probably, would have thought of denying the importance of inward motive, but to go the length that Jesus went aroused suspicion in the minds of those who were strenuously endeavouring to hold a society together by means of an overt and recognized moral discipline. How are you to know whether or not a man is a good, law-abiding Jew, unless by what he *does*, whatever may be in his mind or heart? The suspicion might well seem justified by the encouragement Jesus gave to people who were conspicuously not good, law-abiding Jews—the 'publicans and sinners' of the Synoptics, 'this rabble that cares nothing for the Law', as the Pharisees call them in the Fourth Gospel (Jn. vii. 49).

Now the question may be raised—has been raised by modern scholars—whether the words and actions of Jesus did in fact amount to repudiation of the Law. It was open to argument, and the controversial dialogues of the gospels show that Jesus was prepared to argue the question. But his critics rightly divined that his whole approach was radically different from theirs, and ultimately destructive of their aims. Carried to its logical issue it meant that the *halakha*, the system of rules by which the Law was to be made applicable to every possible situation, was no longer central, and no longer the sufficient guide to the good life. And this threatened the integrity and distinctiveness of Judaism as a national-religious system. 'The Judaism of that time', a modern Jewish author has written, 'had no other aim than to save the tiny nation, the guardian of great ideals, from sinking into the broad sea of heathen culture, and enable it, slowly and gradually, to realize the teaching of the Prophets in civil life and in the present world of the Jewish state and nation.'[1]

This aim, moreover, was being pursued in a situation in which resentment of pagan domination, and national sensitiveness, were mounting towards the fatal climax of A.D. 66. We have to allow for something approaching a war-mentality among large sections of the Jewish people—and we know how that can affect one's judgment. It was not clear to those who kept watch upon him that Jesus really cared for the national cause. When he was told about Pilate's slaughter of Galilaeans in the temple, he responded, not with indignant denunciation of Roman brutality, but with a warning to his own people to 'repent' (Lk. xiii. 1–2). While the zealous sectaries of Qumran were exhorted to 'love all the children of light and hate all the children of darkness',[2] Jesus said, 'Love your enemies.'

In this kind of atmosphere, even if all his alleged deviations from rabbinic orthodoxy put together may not have amounted to anything like a criminal offence, at any rate a capital offence, we can well understand that he came to be surrounded with

---

[1] J. Klausner, *Jesus of Nazareth* (Eng. tr. Allen & Unwin, 1925), p. 376.

[2] *Manual of Discipline* (ed. Eduard Löhse, 1964), I. 9–10.

a cloud of suspicion and prejudice which might condense and solidify dangerously. And if the content of his teaching awakened suspicion, still more did the way in which he presented it. If Mark notes that he taught with a note of authority, he is only putting into a few words what any observant reader of the Sayings can see for himself, from their form, style and general tone. The characteristic formula is not the rabbinic 'It is written', nor even the prophetic 'Thus saith the Lord', but λέγω ὑμῖν, 'I tell you', often introduced by the emphatic ἀμήν, which is said to be an entirely unique use of the word.

Here, it seemed, was one who pitted his own judgment against the massive weight of authority drawn from a tradition built up through centuries. 'Moses received the Law from Sinai, and he delivered it to Joshua, and Joshua to the Elders, and the Elders to the Prophets, and the Prophets to the men of the Great Synagogue.' So begins the Mishnaic tractate *Pirqe Aboth*, and it goes on to trace the impressive pedigree, generation by generation, to Hillel and Shammai and their successors, some of whom were active contemporaries of Jesus. Could such men fail to be affronted by the authority with which he spoke? Could they help asking, 'Who does he think he is?'

He proclaimed with prophetic assurance the coming of the kingdom of God, with its promise of judgment and renewal. But not only so, he spoke as if he himself stood at the centre of this divine event. He declared (in a saying which is almost certainly authentic, although Mark throws doubt upon it) that it was he who should build the new temple[1]—or in other words constitute the new Israel, the final people of God. He pronounced the doom of the Last Judgment on the unrepentant cities of Galilee (Matt. xi. 21–4, Lk. x. 12–15), and he declared that by their attitude to him his contemporaries would be judged 'before the angels of God' (Lk. xii. 8). Similarly (since acquittal as well as condemnation belongs to the office of a

---

[1] Mk. xiv. 57–9. The fact that the saying occurs in variant forms in Matt. xxvi. 60–1, Jn. ii. 19, does not tell against its substantial authenticity. It may be, as Mark says, that the version he quotes as that of the false witnesses was inaccurate, but that Jesus did say something to this effect is certain.

judge) he took upon himself to pronounce the forgiveness of
sins; upon which they commented, 'This is blasphemy!'

And so we come back to the question I postponed; what was
the blasphemy for which Jesus is said to have been condemned?
In the *pericopé* of Mark (ii. 3–12) to which I refer, the healing
of paralysis and the forgiveness of sins are the same action on
two planes: the overt effect: 'Take up your bed and walk'; the
inward reality: 'Your sins are forgiven.' Now according to a
saying reported in Matthew and Luke the miracles of Jesus
were performed by the Spirit, or the finger, of God, and were
a function of the coming of the kingdom of God (Matt. xii. 28,
Lk. xi. 20). His adversaries denied it, and said they were
inspired by the devil—much as in *Bab. Sanh.* he is said to have
practised sorcery. To say this, according to Mark (iii. 8), was
to blaspheme the Holy Spirit; as if the charge of blasphemy
were retorted upon the accusers. In truth, the evangelists
would have us perceive, healing and forgiveness, with power
for the one and authority for the other—two aspects of the
same thing—are divine operations; they are 'works of God',
as John has it.

And it is interesting to trace a similar concatenation of ideas
in the Fourth Gospel, within a very different theological
ambience. The healing at the Pool of Bethesda is, by implication, an act of forgiveness, for Jesus addresses his patient in
the words, 'Look! Now you are well. Don't sin again, or worse
may befall you!' Then there develops an argument (Jn. v.
17–30) starting from the proposition, 'My Father has never
yet ceased his work, and I am working too', upon which the
critics base a charge that Jesus, by calling God his own Father
(τὸν ἴδιον πατέρα, as distinct, perhaps, from the sense in
which he was the Father of all Israelites), has 'claimed equality
with God'. This charge Jesus rebuts, while affirming that he
is indeed doing the works of God—which are judgment and
the giving of life (κρίνειν and ζῳοποιεῖν). How readily these
functions associate themselves with the acts of healing and
forgiveness reported in the Synoptics is evident enough. A
similar charge is brought in another passage of the Fourth
Gospel, x. 22–38, a passage pervaded, indeed, with the special
Johannine theology, but still turning upon the same central

group of ideas. 'I have set before you many good deeds,' says Jesus, 'done by my Father's power; for which of these would you stone me?' 'Not for any good deed,' his critics reply, 'but for blasphemy.' 'Why do you charge me with blasphemy for saying "I am God's son"?'

The evangelists, I conclude, John and the Synoptics alike, take the view that Jesus was charged with blasphemy because he spoke and acted in ways which implied that he stood in a special relation with God, so that his words carried divine authority and his actions were instinct with divine power. Unless this could be believed, the implied claim was an affront to the deepest religious sentiments of his people, a profanation of sanctities; and this, I suggest, is what the charge of 'blasphemy' really stands for, rather than any definable statutory offence. In the stylized account of the examination before the Sanhedrin the key phrases are 'Son of the Blessed' and 'at the right hand of God', which contain within themselves the essential purport of the linked ideas we have been exploring. Whether or not Jesus had put himself forward as Messiah, the implied claim was messianic at least, perhaps rather messianic *plus*. The messianic idea, as it can be gathered—far from precisely or consistently—from the Old Testament and relevant Jewish sources, overlaps, but does not by any means coincide, with the gospel portrayal of the status and mission of Jesus. If the High Priest succeeded, as he seems to have done, in extorting from his Prisoner an admission that he did claim to be Messiah, in some sense, this was more serviceable as a basis for a quasi-political charge than as being in itself a ground of condemnation for technical blasphemy. Such at least is the suggestion which I would put forward.

On this reading of the gospel *data* it becomes credible and intelligible that the Pharisees, among whom Jesus might have been expected to find allies—among whom he did indeed find some sympathizers, as the gospels more than hint—turned against him for the most part, and formed an alliance, strictly temporary and *ad hoc*, with their natural enemies, the Sadducees; and it was this alliance that opened the way to his condemnation and death. It is hardly likely that the Sadducaic hierarchy, under the leadership of Annas and Caiaphas, were deeply

moved by the religious and moral considerations that counted
with the Pharisees. But they were the guardians of the *status
quo*, in a situation where relations between the Jewish nation
and the paramount power were increasingly delicate. Anything
that savoured of popular messianism endangered those relations. The priests may have heard rumours that Jesus had
been mixed up with the resistance movement in Galilee, which,
John says, at one point wished to make him king (vi. 15).
At any rate he rode into Jerusalem acclaimed by a crowd
chanting nationalist slogans, and his high-handed action in
expelling the permitted traders from the Court of the Gentiles,
to all appearance with popular support, was a challenge to the
legal custodians of the sacred area. 'By what authority do you
act like this?' they demanded, and he refused to answer, except
in terms which tacitly implied that his authority was of divine
origin—ἐξ οὐρανοῦ (Mk. xi. 27–33). It was the conflict about
authority over again, on a different level. If we reflect on the
significance of this far-reaching claim to authority, we may
possibly guess at a reason why Jesus was not prepared to deny
that he was a king; for the essence of kingship is authority.

The hierarchy had resolved, as I take it, that Jesus was too
dangerous to be allowed to live. They were able to secure the
indispensable support of the Pharisees, who may have been
able to command a majority in the Sanhedrin, for the reasons
I have suggested. So they could now proceed to act, by citing
Jesus before the Roman governor as a messianic pretender.
But he appeared to have strong backing among the populace.
If the hierarchy let it appear that they were betraying a popular
leader, a possible Messiah, to the heathen power, they would
be in an invidious position. Hence, I suggest, the prominence
given to the charge of blasphemy, the religious charge which
brought the Pharisees into action. The public must see that
Jesus was a criminal legally convicted, by the highest court of
the nation, of a serious religious offence. How far, even so,
they could count on a genuine popular reaction against him
was by no means certain. All through, their assumption seems
to be that the people were on his side. It is true that when there
was a danger that after all the Prisoner might be acquitted,
the priests, so we are told, stirred up the mob to demand the

penalty of crucifixion (Mk. xv. 9–13, Matt. xxvii. 20–22). The experience of recent years has shown how easy it is for an influential group to stage a 'spontaneous' popular demonstration. Whether the outcry before Pilate's tribunal meant anything more than that remains doubtful. At any rate the hierarchy got their way. But the prefect had the last word. The *titulus* affixed to the cross was a calculated insult flung in the face of the priests by the cynical Roman: 'King of the Jews.' At this point theology takes over, and declares, not without some historical warrant, '*Dominus regnavit a ligno.*'

8 The Appearances of the Risen Christ: An Essay in Form-Criticism of the Gospels

The form-critics distinguish with some unanimity two main types of narrative in the gospels. Their nomenclature differs, but if we say that there is a concise and a circumstantial type of narrative, we shall beg no questions. There are no doubt types which do not readily fit either category; there are border-line cases, and it may not be easy, or even possible, to draw the line quite definitely; but anyone can feel the difference in character between, let us say, the story of the Withered Hand or of the Blessing of the Children, and the stories of the Epileptic Boy and the Gadarene Swine. The latter trace the course of an incident from stage to stage with heightening interest, and make it vivid to the reader by means of arresting details, and traits of character in the actors and interlocutors. In the story of the Epileptic we are shown, for example, the embarrassment of the disciples, the alarming symptoms of the boy's disease, the pathos of the father's repeated appeals, the pressure of the crowd, and the suspense created by the difficulty and apparent initial failure of the cure. In the story of the Gadarene Swine we have the horrifying description of the manacled maniac among the tombs, his grotesque fantasy about a legion of devils, the wild stampede of the pigs, the alarm of their owners, and finally the telling contrast of the restored madman, now 'clothed and in his right mind', aspiring to be one of the disciples of Jesus. All such details are a part of the art and craft of the story-teller, who, himself excited by the story he tells, seeks to kindle the imagination of his auditors. These stories are sometimes labelled '*Novellen*', for which, perhaps, the best English equivalent is 'Tales'.

In sharp contrast to these 'tales', the 'concise' type of narrative tells us nothing which is not absolutely essential to a bare report of what happened or what was said. It observes the unities of time and place, and takes no account of development. The situation presupposed is depicted in the fewest possible words ('He went into a synagogue and taught', 'It happened that he was in the house', or the like). Then follows the word or action which set things moving ('There was a man with a withered hand', 'They brought children to him', etc.) and this evokes the significant act or word of Jesus, after which the narrative ends by indicating the response of the interlocutors, or the effect produced upon spectators. This extremely concise and economical style of narrative has been shown by comparison with similar 'forms' elsewhere, to be characteristic of folk-tradition, in which an oft-repeated story is rubbed down and polished, like a water-worn pebble, until nothing but the essential remains, in its most arresting and memorable form. And it is a form which makes it possible for the story to be told as a self-contained unit, without any necessary direct link with what precedes or follows. The inference is that narratives of this 'concise' type (which should be made to include not only 'Pronouncement-stories' or 'Apophthegms', but also stories of action, such as 'Miracle-stories', cast in a similar mould) are drawn directly from the oral tradition handed down by the corporate memory of the Church, and consequently that they belong to a deposit which was deeply cherished and constantly repeated because it was bound up with the central interests of the Christian community.

The 'Tales' on the contrary allow more room for the taste and ability of the individual narrator. They are closer to the 'unformed', or free, body of reminiscences which must have floated about in early Christian circles. That they were in consequence more exposed to alteration or 'improvement' is no doubt true; but I can see no cogent reason for accepting the view that the 'Tales' as a body represent a later, or secondary stage of the tradition.[1] If they are said to include 'worldly'

---

[1] Contrast the relatively 'concise' narratives of Matt. viii. 28–34, ix. 18–26, with the 'circumstantial' narratives of Mk. v. 1–20, 21–43. Few critics would assign the former to an earlier date. If Matthew,

traits, were the Christians so insulated from the world, even in the earliest days, that they had no interest in a well-told tale?

These two types of narrative which have been distinguished in the evangelical records of the ministry of Jesus may be recognized also in those parts of the gospels which follow upon the account of the discovery of the empty Tomb on Easter morning. Here we are given a number of narratives of appearances of the risen Christ to certain of his followers. Some of these narratives have a character similar to that of the 'Tales'. For example, the stories of the Walk to Emmaus in Lk. xxiv, and of the meal by the Sea of Galilee in Jn. xxi, are full of the kind of dramatic detail and characterization which we have noted in such stories as those of the Epileptic Boy and the Gadarene Swine. On the other hand there are other narratives which equally clearly show the traits of such 'concise' narratives as the Withered Hand and the Blessing of the Children.

It will be well to start by analysing these 'concise' narratives. If we take, to begin with, the appearances of Christ to the Women in Matt. xxviii. 8–10, to 'the Eleven Disciples' in Matt. xxviii. 16–20, and to 'the Disciples' in Jn. xx. 19–21, it is easy to recognize a common pattern, which we may analyse as follows:

A. The situation: Christ's followers bereft of their Lord.
B. The appearance of the Lord.
C. The Greeting.
D. The Recognition.
E. The Word of Command.

I shall label narratives of this type, Class I, and those of the circumstantial' type, Class II.

---

in ix. 27–31 and xx. 29–34, has taken over two forms of a story, the one more 'concise' and the other more 'circumstantial', there is no ground for making either the one or the other 'primary' or 'secondary': they are simply variant forms which the tradition assumed.

Class I

We must now examine the three examples of 'concise' narrative, to see how the common pattern is variously developed. Using the index letters employed above, we get the following scheme:

	MATT. xxviii. 8–10	MATT. xxviii. 16–20	JN. xx. 19–21
A.	The Women were on the way from the Tomb to the Disciples.	The Eleven Disciples went to Galilee, to the Mountain appointed as rendezvous.	Late on Sunday evening the Disciples were gathered with closed doors [for fear of the Jews].
B.	Jesus met them.	Jesus approached.	Jesus stood in the midst.
C.	He said Χαίρετε.[1]	—	He said Εἰρήνη ὑμῖν.[1]
D.	They approached, grasped His feet, and did Him reverence.	When they saw Him they did reverence, though some doubted.	The disciples were very glad when they saw the Lord.
E.	Go and announce to my brothers that they are to go to Galilee and they will see me there.	Go and make disciples of all nations ...	As the Father sent me, so I send you.

It is to be observed that the bare pattern is expanded at certain points, but in so brief a way as not to alter the character of the *pericopé*. The expansions add nothing fresh, but emphasize what is already present in the pattern, though scarcely explicit. Thus, in all three *pericopae* there is at least a hint of an element of doubt or fear. In Matt. xxviii. 17 it is explicit: 'some doubted'. In Matt. xxviii. 10 it is implied in the words, 'Fear not'. In Jn. xx. 20 nothing is said of any doubt in the minds of the disciples, but the Lord 'showed them his hands and his side', thus setting at rest, by proof tendered, a doubt which was there though unexpressed. Neither of the Matthaean *pericopae* has any such explicit tender of proof. In xxviii. 18 the words of

---

[1] *Χαίρετε* is the normal everyday greeting in Greek; εἰρήνη ὑμῖν represents the normal greeting in Hebrew or Aramaic. If we may suppose an Aramaic tradition underlying, the word might well be the same in both.

H

the Lord, 'All authority is given to me', seem sufficient to set all doubts at rest, but in xxviii. 9 the fact that the women touch his feet may be held to carry an implicit assurance that there is a real Person before them. It is perhaps legitimate to say that this type of resurrection narrative carries within it, as an integral element, a suggestion that the appearance of the Lord does not bring full or immediate conviction to the beholders, who require some form of assurance: the sight of his wounds, contact with his body, or his word of authority.

Each *pericopé* works up (like the 'Paradigms' or 'Pronouncement-stories') to a significant word of the Lord. In Matt. xxviii. 10 it is no more than an injunction to the disciples to keep their rendezvous in Galilee. In Jn. xx. 21 it is a formal commission to the apostles, in its simplest form: 'As the Father sent me, so I send you.' After this a second incident is added: the 'Insufflation', accompanied by a further charge. This however is strictly not a part of the narrative of the appearance of the Lord: the gift of the Spirit is a separate incident, even though, in John's setting of the story, it follows immediately upon the Christophany. In Matt. xxviii. 18–20 the commission is given a more extended form, covering a wider field: the mission to the nations; the ordinance of baptism; the threefold Name; the promise of the Lord's perpetual presence. Here the standard pattern of resurrection-narrative has been used to introduce a kind of 'church-order', which may be compared with the 'church-order' of Matt. xviii. 15–20.

Allowing, then, for these minimal supplements, we may recognize a standard pattern of resurrection-*pericopé* which is analogous to that of the 'concise' narratives in the accounts of the Ministry, and like them bears the marks of a tradition shaped, and rubbed down to essentials, in the process of oral transmission. Two of them are so formed that they are complete in themselves. 'The Eleven went to a mountain in Galilee' is just such an opening as 'They entered into a synagogue', or 'He went to Capernaum'; and 'On Sunday evening when the doors were shut where the disciples were . . .' is comparable with 'In those days when there was a great crowd and they had nothing to eat'. In Matt. xxviii. 8 there is no similar beginning: a connection exists with what has preceded; yet the *pericopé* might have stood alone, and comparison with Mark shows that there has in any case been some editorial manipulation hereabouts.

We must ask later whether there are any other *pericopae* which, though not reproducing the pattern in so pure a form, properly belong to the same class; but for the moment it will be better to turn to those which clearly belong to a different class, that of 'circumstantial' narratives.

Class II

Here we have two obvious examples to start with: the Walk to Emmaus in Lk. xxiv. 13–35, and the Appearance by the Sea in Jn. xxi. 1–14.

1. The Walk to Emmaus is a highly-finished literary composition, in which the author, dwelling with loving interest upon every detail of his theme, has lost no opportunity of evoking an imaginative response in the reader. The pace of the story is leisurely, and the lapse of time is marked. The walk, enlivened by absorbing conversation, continues until we find that time has slipped by and the day is far spent. The return journey to Jerusalem is felt by contrast to be hurried, and interest passes at once to the reunion of the travellers with the Eleven, and the interchange of startling news. The changing moods of the two companions are convincingly rendered; their encounter with the unknown Stranger and their invitation to him to break his journey are managed with admirable naturalness; the scene of recognition at the supper-table, with the immediate disappearance of the mysterious Guest, is dramatically effective. We observe also the precise identification of persons and places: the name of one of the travellers, Cleopas; the village of Emmaus, sixty *stades* from Jerusalem. All these are not traits of a corporate tradition. They are characteristic of the practised story-teller, who knows just how to 'put his story across'.

But further, the writer has used the captivating narrative as a setting for a comprehensive treatment of the theme of Christ's resurrection in its character of a reunion of the Lord with his followers. The dialogue is so managed that it leads up to a basic programme for the study of 'testimonies' from the Old Testament, which was the foundation of the earliest theological enterprise of the primitive Church.[1] The recognition of the Lord at table carries a significant suggestion to a community which made the 'breaking of bread' the centre of its fellowship. Not only so: the narrative is so contrived as to include, by means of 'flash-backs', the discovery of the empty Tomb, the angelic announcement, and the appearance of the Lord to Peter (xxiv. 22–4, 34), so that the *pericopé* as a whole forms a kind of summary 'Gospel of the Resurrection'.

It is clear, then, that we have no mere expansion of the general pattern, but a carefully-composed statement, which, in the framework of a narrative of intense dramatic interest, includes most of what (from this evangelist's point of view) needs to be said about the resurrection of Christ. It is however worth noting that here, as elsewhere, the story begins with the disciples feeling the loss of their Lord, that Jesus takes the initiative, and that the dramatic centre of the whole incident is the ἀναγνώρισις—for it seems proper in this case to use the technical term applied by ancient literary critics to the recognition-scene which was so often the crucial point of a Greek drama.[2]

2. The account of the appearance of the Lord to seven disciples by the Sea of Galilee, contained in the appendix to the Fourth Gospel (Jn. xxi. 1–14), is recorded within the framework of a complex narrative, covering a considerable lapse of time from the evening of one day, all through the night, to the morning of a second day. The narrative comprises two

---

[1] Cf. xxiv. 46–7, Acts xxvi. 22–3, where we have a primitive scheme for biblical research. It is scarcely accidental that Cleopas is represented as having sought in Jesus the fulfilment of the (political) hope of the ἀπολύτρωσις of Israel, and that he learns instead that it is through suffering that the Messiah must enter into a glory which is clearly not of this world.

[2] See the admirable discussion of forms of ἀναγνώρισις in Aristotle, *De Arte Poetica*, 16, pp. 1454b.19–1455a.21 Aristotle's distinctions of various methods of recognition may be aptly applied to the New Testament material.

distinct but interlocking incidents: the fishing of the disciples and breakfast on the shore. Each is told with a wealth of picturesque detail. The incidents are dramatic, the dialogue lively and in character. There is abundant detail. We learn, for example, not only that Peter impulsively leapt into the sea, but that he first put on his coat; not only that a fire was kindled on the beach and breakfast prepared, but that it was a charcoal fire and that bread and fish were supplied. We are told the number of the company, five of whom are identified, the distance of the boat from shore, and the number of fish,[1] which strained the net but did not break it. All this is strictly unnecessary to the main theme. It is characteristic of the story-teller, and reflects his interest in the story and his mastery of his craft. The centre of interest is the recognition of the risen Lord, but here the recognition is not immediate but spread over an appreciable period. It begins with the dramatic exclamation of the beloved disciple, which impels Peter to jump overboard, but it is not complete until the party has landed and Jesus, having invited them to breakfast, distributes bread and fish. The motive of the breaking of bread appears once again, as in the Emmaus story. There is evidence in early Christian art that the meal of the seven disciples was treated, along with the Feeding of the Multitude, as a symbol of the Eucharist.

Unlike Lk. xxiv. 13–35, the *pericopé* does not embody didactic passages in the story itself, which is a straightforward, uninterrupted, dramatic narrative. But it is made to lead up to a significant dialogue, in the course of which Peter receives his apostolic commission. Thus the motive of Matt. xxviii. 19 and Jn. xx. 21 reappears in a different setting. In spite of the marked contrast in form and pattern, we are still in close contact with the fundamental motives which underlie the concise narratives of Class I.

We have now established the fact of two clearly distinguishable types of resurrection narrative. We must next examine the

---

[1] Fantastic applications of *gematria* to the number are out of place, but it is probably significant that some zoologists of the period computed the number of species of fishes as 153.

remaining such narratives in the gospels, which appear to be doubtful or intermediate types, to see to which of the two main classes they are more akin. They are as follows:

1. The appearance to 'the Eleven' in the Received Text of Mark. Mk. xvi. 14–15.
2. The appearance to 'the Eleven and those with them' in Lk. xxiv. 36–49.
3. Mary Magdalen at the Tomb in Jn. xx. 11–17.
4. Doubting Thomas. Jn. xx. 26–9.

1. The so-called 'Longer Ending' of Mark must no doubt be regarded as 'spurious' in the sense that it formed no part of the Gospel according to Mark as it originally appeared; but as a rendering of the early Christian tradition of the resurrection appearances it demands consideration on its merits. On the face of it the *pericopé* conforms fairly closely to the type of Class I.

A. As the Eleven were sitting (at table) cf. Lk. xxiv. 30, Jn. xxi. 13.
B. Jesus appeared to them.
C. (In place of Greeting.) He reproached them for incredulity.
D. [The Recognition is wanting, though implied.]
E. He said 'Go into all the world and preach the Gospel. . . .'

The *pericopé* thus culminates, like Matt. xxviii. 16–20, Jn. xx. 19–21, in a commission to the apostles, which is also represented in the dialogue which follows on Jn. xxi. 1–14; and here, as elsewhere, it develops beyond the immediate situation into a more general instruction to the Church, with the promise of divine assistance.

The question may be raised, whether this *pericopé* is based (as parts of the 'Longer Ending' almost certainly are) upon the narratives in the canonical gospels. That the Eleven were at table when Christ appeared to them is a trait which does not appear elsewhere: in Lk. xxiv. 30 it is two disciples (apparently alluded to in Mk. xvi. 12), neither of them belonging to the apostolic body, to whom he is known in the breaking of bread; and in Jn. xxi. 13 it is a body of seven disciples, two of whom are unidentified, to whom he distributes bread and fish. It is therefore no more likely that the author of the Longer Ending took this trait from the canonical gospels than that it is an independent rendering of a traditional motif. The incredulity of the Eleven—or rather of some of them—is referred to in Matt. xxviii. 17, and, as we have seen, it may be taken to be implied in the tendering of proofs in Jn. xx. 20. But nowhere else does Christ, instead of greeting his disciples, reproach them. Thomas indeed is reproached, by implication, in Jn. xx. 26-7, and the two companions in Lk. xxiv. 25, but the (rest of the) Eleven are not implicated. Thus it is not improbable that we have, here again, a generalized trait in the current tradition finding independent expression in a particular formulation of the tradition. In short, it appears reasonably likely that Mk. xvi. 14-15 is to be added to Class I, as another example of the formulation of tradition in a 'concise' narrative. In that sense it would be a 'genuine' record, in spite of its dubious credentials, since it adheres closely to the general traditional pattern without slavishly following any other written account known to us.

2. Lk. xxiv. 36-49. We have here a *pericopé* of mixed character. The main items in the pattern of 'concise' narratives re-appear, though much modified:

A. They were talking together.
B. Jesus stood in the midst (cf. Jn. xx. 19).
C. [He said 'Peace to you', as in Jn. xx. 19; but not in the 'Western Text'.]
D. The process of recognition is greatly spun out: at first the disciples are terrified (cf. Matt. xxviii. 10), and think they are seeing a ghost: Jesus tenders proof by pointing to his hands and feet (cf. Jn. xx. 20) and invites them to touch him (cf. Jn. xx. 27). They are still incredulous, and he tenders final proof by eating in their presence.
E. The concluding word of command is here replaced by a longish address consisting of (*a*) instruction regarding the use of testimonies from the Old Testament (cf. Lk. xxiv. 26-7), (*b*) a commission to preach (cf. Matt. xxviii. 19), and (*c*) the assurance of the help of the Spirit (cf. Jn. xx. 22-3, Matt. xxviii. 20, where the presence of Christ is equivalent).

It is clear that we have here an extensive working-over of the common pattern. In most of the *pericopae* that we have studied,

the proofs of identity are hardly more than hinted at. Only in
Jn. xx. 20 are we explicitly told that Christ pointed to his
wounds. In the present *pericopé* the corresponding statement
(Lk. xxiv. 40) is not certainly part of the original text, but there
is a formal pronouncement of Christ which makes the point
far more emphatic: 'Look at my hands and feet [and convince
yourselves] that it is I myself.' And whereas in Matt. xxviii. 9
the women clasp the Lord's feet in a spontaneous gesture of
devotion, here he bids them 'Feel me, and look; a ghost has
not flesh and bones, as you see that I have'. Again, whereas in
the 'Longer Ending' of Mark the Lord appears to the Eleven
at table, and in the Emmaus story and the Appendix to the
Fourth Gospel he is known to his followers in the breaking
of bread, here he asks for food, and clinches the proof that a
real Person is before them by actually eating broiled fish in
their presence—a unique feature in the gospel narratives,
though it may be intended by the not quite clear statements of
Acts i. 4, x. 41.

The *pericopé* is thus no longer a simple, traditional story of
the appearance of the Lord: it is a piece of controversial
apologetic set in the framework of such a story. The simpler
narratives conveyed something of the naïve, spontaneous sense
of the primitive believers that something almost too good to
be true has happened. Here we are aware of something different: the faith must be defended by argument, not against the
natural doubts of simple people, but against a reflective and
sophisticated scepticism. Yet it would not be right to class this
pericopé with the 'Tales'. There is no detail in the narrative
(with one exception) which is not strictly necessary to it as a
piéce justificative. The one exception is the statement that the
Lord ate broiled fish.[1] It would have been sufficient for the
narrator's immediate purpose to affirm that Christ ate food in
the presence of his disciples. The added detail is the kind of
trait that marks the story-teller. For the rest, it is enough to
compare the details of this *pericopé* with those of the Walk to
Emmaus and the Appearance by the Sea of Galilee to be con-

---

[1] Some MSS., entering into the spirit of the scene, add 'and
honeycomb'.

vinced that it does not belong to Class II. It may perhaps best be characterized as an example of the 'concise' type of narrative in which apologetic motives have caused everything else to be subordinated to an elaborate presentation, not indeed of the ἀναγνώρισις itself, but of the grounds upon which such recognition was based.[1] It is certainly more remote from the original tradition, orally handed down, than the typical narratives of Class I, but the obvious work of an author has not altogether disguised the form of the tradition which underlies.

3. Jn. xx. 11–17. The story of the appearance of Christ to Mary Magdalen at the Tomb on Easter morning is told briefly and with great economy of words. So far it would seem natural to include it among the 'concise' narratives of Class I. The evangelist has indeed so woven the theme of the appearance with that of the angelic announcement that the kind of opening which is normal in narratives of this class is obscured, but apart from this, it is easy enough to recognize the typical pattern.

A. Mary stood by the Tomb.
B. Jesus appeared.
C. He greeted her.
D. She recognized Him.
E. He gave her a command.

But when we have said this, it is obvious that we have something very different from the regular examples of 'concise' narrative. In spite of all the brevity and economy, the narrator has succeeded in conveying, not so much incidents as psychological traits, which are not necessary to the presentation of the main theme, but appeal to the imagination. Mary stood weeping. She turned suddenly round and saw a Figure whom she took for the gardener. The reader's attention is at once arrested. There follows a dialogue as richly suggestive as it is brief. The two speeches with which it ends, one from each of the interlocutors, consist of one word each: 'Mary'—'Rabbuni!'

[1] The production of multiple proofs of identity is a familiar accompaniment of the ἀναγνώρισις motive in Greek drama, both tragic and comic.

Yet they are laden with meaning. The words which Christ then
utters have the character of Johannine theology, as the distinctive use of the verb ἀναβαίνειν[1] sufficiently indicates. In their
present form, at least, they are no doubt the composition of the
evangelist. But in this John has done no differently from the
other evangelists, who, as we have seen, hold themselves free

---

[1] This verb has a special significance in the vocabulary of the
Fourth Gospel, e.g. iii. 13–17, vi. 62–3. So pregnant is it that there
is reason to suspect that even where, ostensibly, it means no more
than the journey of a pilgrim to the Holy City, it is intended to
carry overtones. If so, then it is not altogether unlikely that the
message to the 'brothers' of Jesus here intentionally alludes to what
he is recorded to have said to his 'brothers' in vii. 3–8. They have
urged him to go to Jerusalem to make a public appeal. He replies,
'My time is not yet here. . . . I am not "going up"—οὐκ (or ?
οὔπω) ἀναβαίνω—to this feast, because my time is not yet ripe'. With
that in mind, we might read the message which Mary is to carry to
the 'brothers' as meaning, 'My time is now ripe; I am "going up"—
not to Jerusalem, but to my Father'. It is perhaps significant that it is
only in the accounts of the appearance to Mary Magdalen here, and
to the women (one of whom, at least editorially, is Mary Magdalen)
in Matt. xxviii. 9–10, that account is taken of the 'brothers' of
Christ in recounting his resurrection. In Mk. xvi. 7 the message is
sent to 'his disciples and Peter'. In Lk. xxiv. 33–5 the news is
given to 'the Eleven and those with them'. In Lk. xxiv. 22 the 'we'
who receive the angelic announcement from the women are indeterminate, and equally indeterminate are the expressions used in the
'Longer Ending' of Mk. xvi. 10, 13. Now in the early Church the
'brothers' of Jesus were a well-recognized group (cf. I Cor. ix. 5),
who long enjoyed a special position in the Church as Founder's kin.
The leading member of the group was James. We know from I Cor.
xv. 7 that an appearance of the Lord to James was affirmed in the
primitive tradition, though it is nowhere recorded in the canonical
Gospels. Is it possible (this is pure speculation) that the report of an
appearance to Mary Magdalen and other women was especially
associated with the tradition of James and his circle, and that this
tradition was largely eclipsed by the tradition preserved in the circle
of Peter and the Twelve? Cf. also Acts i. 14.

to expand or develop the concluding utterance of the Lord, in order to make it a vehicle for some significant summary of his purpose for his Church. Yet even so, the 'Touch me not!' has a dramatic value in the story quite independent of its theological import.

These features all tend to associate the present *pericopé* with the 'circumstantial' narratives of Class II. They are quite alien from the ethos of folk-tradition, to which belongs a certain naïveté evident in all our 'concise' narratives. There is nothing naïve here, but a reflective, subtle, most delicate approach to the depths of human experience. This story never came out of any common stock of tradition; it has an arresting individuality. We seem to be shut up to two alternatives. Either we have here a free, imaginative composition based upon the bare tradition of an appearance to Mary Magdalen, akin to that represented by Matt. xxviii. 9–10, or else the story came through some highly individual channel directly from the source, and the narrator stood near enough to catch the *nuances* of the original experience. It would be hazardous to dogmatize. The power to render psychological traits imaginatively, with convincing insight, cannot be denied to a writer to whom we owe the masterly character-parts of Pontius Pilate and the Woman of Samaria. Yet I confess that I cannot for long rid myself of the feeling (it can be no more than a feeling) that this *pericopé* has something indefinably first-hand about it. It stands in any case alone. There is nothing quite like it in the gospels. Is there anything quite like it in all ancient literature?

4. Jn. xx. 26–9. The story of Doubting Thomas is a pendant to the 'concise' narrative of the appearance to the disciples in xx. 19–21 (see pp. 105–107 above). It hardly forms a separable *pericopé*, for it is not fully intelligible without the connecting narrative of xx. 24–5. Its theological and apologetic motives are obvious. Its broad pattern scarcely differs from that of our typical 'concise' narratives of Class I, and there is little in the way of picturesque detail (not directly demanded by the main motive) to associate it with the 'circumstantial' narratives of Class II. Thomas is hardly an individual as Mary Magdalen is; he is a type of the 'some' who 'doubted', according to Matt. xxviii. 17. We should not be far wrong in saying that John has

chosen to split up the composite traditional picture of a group some of whom recognize the Lord while others doubt, and to give contrasting pictures of the believers and the doubter, in order to make a point which is essentially theological. The Thomas-*pericopé* has its nearest analogue in Lk. xxiv. 36–43, but it is at once farther removed in character from the primitive tradition and far more delicate and perceptive in approach.

We have now surveyed all the narratives of appearances of the Lord in the canonical gospels, which seem to have any claim to be treated as separate units of tradition, whether they belong to the class of 'concise' narratives reflecting directly the corporate tradition of the primitive Church, or to the class of 'circumstantial' narratives allowing more scope to the individual author, or whether they diverge in various ways from both types.

Outside the canonical gospels there is little that we can bring into comparison. We have three accounts of the appearance of Christ to Paul, but none of the three constitutes a narrative unit comparable with those which provide the material of the gospels. The narrative, in all its forms, resembles those of the gospels in so far that the word of Christ initiates the transaction, that the recognition is the central feature, and that the scene ends with a command of Christ. But the whole situation is so different[1] that the comparison is of little significance.

In Rev. i. 10–18 we have an 'appearance' of Christ to John in Patmos described in apocalyptic terms, with all the usual imagery. Comparison with the gospel narratives is not profitable, except to underline the fact that the latter are entirely free from these apocalyptic traits. Even where, as in Matt. xxviii. 16–20, the intention is clearly to introduce the risen Christ as

[1] The story of the conversion of Paul is avowedly an episode in the life of an individual who has a biography of his own. Of the persons recorded as having followed Jesus in his lifetime, the only one who is (in even approximately the same sense) an individual with a biography is Peter, and the appearance to Peter is nowhere described.

King of the World, seated upon the throne of his glory (cf. Matt. xxv. 31–4), there is no attempt to suggest that glory through the conventional symbolism of apocalypse. The gospel narratives, indeed, are notably sober and almost matter-of-fact in tone.

Outside the New Testament there is little of which we need take note. The Gospel according to the Hebrews, so Jerome informs us, contained an account of an appearance to James. The fragments he quotes are not sufficient for any complete reconstruction of the narrative. The situation presupposed appears to be different from anything contemplated in the canonical gospels, for the first fragment reads, 'When the Lord had given the linen cloth to the servant of the priest, he went and appeared to James.' It is then explained that James had taken a vow not to eat bread until he should have seen Jesus risen from the dead, and the narrative goes on to tell how the Lord 'took bread and broke and gave it to James the Just; and said to him "Eat your bread, my brother, for the Son of Man has risen from them that sleep".' The association of the appearance of the Lord with a meal, and in particular with the breaking of bread, we have already noted as a feature of several of the canonical narratives, but for the rest this narrative has little in common with them. Clearly it had more of the character of a 'tale' than of the 'concise' type of narrative drawn from the common oral tradition.

The Gospel of Peter evidently contained at least one narrative of an appearance of the risen Lord. The longest extant fragment (in the Akhmim MS.) ends with what was clearly the beginning of a story about an appearance to Peter and others, who have taken their nets and gone to the sea. We can only conjecture that something similar to Jn. xxi. followed, but to which type of narrative it would conform we have no means of knowing.

The material outside the canonical gospels, then, whether in the New Testament or in apocryphal gospels, is of no great importance for our purpose, but it does give a little help, by comparison and contrast, towards defining the forms in which the tradition of appearances of the risen Lord was preserved. We should now have a fairly clear idea of these forms—of the two main types and of the range of variation from them.

It should have become clear that the skeleton outline which we noted for the 'concise' narratives of Class I remains valid, on the whole, for all the varieties: the 'orphaned' disciples (cf. Jn. xiv. 18); the appearance of the Lord, usually with some word of greeting; the process of recognition; the final word of command. All the additional material in the narratives of Class II is little more than expansion of this general outline. The expansion is usually related either to the plight of the disciples, or to the process of recognition, or to the content of the final word of command, or to two or all three of these. Of actually extraneous matter there is little or nothing.

By this I do not mean that we are to suppose the writers of the 'circumstantial' narratives to have had before them as sources existing narratives of the 'concise' type, which they set about elaborating. To attempt to extract from the story of the Walk to Emmaus or the Appearance by the Sea some original nucleus which would conform to the pattern of Class I would be an unprofitable task. I conceive Class I to represent the 'formed' tradition, stereotyped through relatively long transmission within a community, and Class II to represent a freer and more individual treatment of the still 'unformed' tradition consisting, we may suppose, of things that various people remembered to have seen or to have been told, and in their turn related in a spontaneous and unconstrained fashion. Comparison with material outside the gospels has tended—for what it is worth when there is so little such material—to emphasize by contrast the broad, basic similarity of the gospel narratives among themselves.

There are no further such narratives to be examined. But there are certain *pericopae*, incorporated in the portions of the gospels dealing with the Ministry of Jesus, which have been more or less widely regarded as representing traditions referring originally to post-resurrection appearances of the Lord. It will be of interest to test such *pericopae* by the standard of the established scheme which we have recognized.

1. Lk. v. 1–11: the miraculous Draught of Fishes and the

Call of Peter. The resemblance of this whole *pericopé* to Jn. xxi. has led many critics to suggest that it was originally a post-resurrection narrative, as it is in the Fourth Gospel, and that Luke (or his immediate authority) transplanted the incident into the context of the Ministry—as others have suggested that John transplanted it in the opposite direction. There is certainly a problem here, but it is one which our form-critical study of the post-resurrection appearances does not greatly help to solve. For supposing the story to have referred, in the original tradition, to the period after the resurrection, practically every *formal* feature of post-resurrection narratives has been eliminated. There is no initial separation between Christ and his disciples, no unexpected appearance, no recognition: only the commission to Peter remains as representing the word of command with which such narratives commonly close. The features which are common to Lk. v. and Jn. xxi. (with this one exception) are those which, even as they occur in John, are not *characteristic* of post-resurrection appearances. The problem, therefore, of the true relation between these two narratives must be solved, if at all, by different methods.

2. Jn. vi. 16–21, Mk. vi. 45–51: the Walking on the Water. This *pericopé*, in its Johannine form, shows many of the features of post-resurrection narratives, as will be clear if we try to apply to it our formal scheme.

A. The disciples were at sea and Jesus was not with them.
B. They saw Jesus walking on the sea.
C. (They were afraid, but) Jesus hailed them with a word of reassurance.
D. They were willing to receive him into the boat (i.e. they recognized him).
E. (The word of command is missing: instead, the voyage ends.)

What we have to observe is that this narrative, just as it stands, *could* have occurred among the narratives of the appearances of the risen Christ. It has some similiarities to the story in Jn. xxi.: the disciples are at sea without Jesus; the reunion takes place (apparently) on shore—assuming, that is, that the words ἤθελον λαβεῖν αὐτὸν εἰς τὸ πλοῖον imply that their intention to take Jesus on board was not fulfilled because they found that they

were already in a position to disembark.[1] Nor is there any
feature which would necessarily be out of place in a post-
resurrection narrative—unless we are to understand that the
disciples actually did receive the Lord into the boat; but John
does not in any case say so.

So far, therefore, as the formal character of the *pericopé* goes,
it would be possible to regard it as a post-resurrection narrative
displaced. It conforms in the main to the type of Class I of
such narratives, but the description of the violence of the wind,
and the measurement of the distance from shore (cf. Jn. xi. 8),
might be regarded as approximating to the form of the 'circumstantial' narratives.

It is, however, to be observed that the Marcan rendering of
this incident is farther away from the type of the post-resurrection narratives. In Mark we are not presented at the beginning
with the picture of the 'orphaned' disciples. Instead, we are told
that *Jesus* took leave of them and went to the mountain, from
which point *he saw them* in trouble, and so *went to meet* them
and proposed to pass them by. So far the whole story is told
from the side of Jesus, as it is in no post-resurrection narrative
except that of the appearance to James in the Gospel according
to the Hebrews. Again, Mark says definitely that he entered
the boat, as John does not, and this would be a trait alien from
the general character of the post-resurrection narratives. If we
are to assume that Mark represents the earlier stage of this
narrative, we should be disposed to infer that John had assimilated it to the form of the post-resurrection narratives. But does
Mark, necessarily, in every case, represent a more primitive
stage of tradition than John? I doubt it. There are in this case
some grounds (which I will not here discuss) for believing

---

[1] If it were legitimate to bring Matthew into the comparison, we
should observe that in both stories Peter plunges into the sea to
join the Lord, Matt. xiv. 28–31, Jn. xxi. 7. The reason why he failed
(in Matthew) is that he 'doubted', for Jesus asks, εἰς τί ἐδίστσσας;
cf. Matt. xxviii. 17 (of the Eleven after the resurrection) οἱ δὲ
ἐδίστασαν. It is difficult not to suspect that there had been some
obscure kind of contact between the two traditions at an early
stage.

that John is following an independent tradition which is in some respects more original than Mark's.

The conclusion we should draw, it appears, is that there is so striking a similarity between this *pericopé* and the general type of post-resurrection narrative that it may well be either (*a*) that a traditional narrative originally referring to an appearance of the risen Lord has been transplanted, whether intentionally or not, into a different context, or (*b*) that an incident which originally belonged to the Galilaean Ministry of Jesus has been influenced by the post-resurrection narratives, and has been, particularly in the Fourth Gospel, assimilated in large measure to their form. In coming to a decision between these alternatives, we should have regard to the fact that in Mark and John alike (though in different ways) the incident is firmly welded into its context, more firmly, indeed, than most of the *pericopae* belonging to the Galilaean Ministry.

3. Mk. ix. 2–8, and parallels. The Transfiguration. Among critics of a certain school it has become a dogma that this is an antedated post-resurrection appearance of the Lord. On formal grounds this theory has no support whatever. On the contrary the *pericopé* in question contrasts with the general type of post-resurrection narrative in almost every particular. Let us go through it point by point. (To save space, I shall use the symbols 'T', for the Transfiguration-*pericopé*, and 'R' for the general type of post-resurrection narrative.)

(i) Whereas R invariably starts with the disciples 'orphaned' of the Lord and records a reunion, in T they are together throughout. If the Evangelists were making use of a form of tradition which began with a separation, it would have been easy enough to contrive a setting for it (cf. Jn. vi. 15–16, Mk. vi. 45).

(ii) In R, a word of Jesus always has a significant place, either as greeting, or as reproach, or as command, or as any two or all three of these. In T, he is silent throughout.

(iii) In T, a voice from heaven proclaims the status and dignity of Christ. There is no voice from heaven in R. Only in Rev. i. 10–11 is there a voice (apparently) from heaven, drawing the seer's attention to the vision which he is to see. In the

I

accounts of the appearance to Paul the voice from heaven is that of Christ himself.

(iv) In T, Christ is accompanied by Moses and Elijah; in fact the 'appearance' (ὤφθη αὐτοῖς!) is that of the two personages of antiquity and not of Christ himself (who is there all along). In R, Christ always appears alone (never accompanied, e.g. by the angels who figure as heralds of the resurrection).

(v) In T, Christ is seen by his disciples clothed in visible glory. This trait is conspicuously absent from R in the gospels. Only in Rev. i. 16 is he described as 'shining like the sun in his power', and this, as we have seen, stands quite apart from the gospel tradition. Its absence is perhaps the more remarkable because a dazzling light provides the visible form in which Christ appeared to Paul according to Acts; and since Paul himself includes his own experience in the list of appearances of the risen Lord, there may well have been a temptation to colour other forms of R accordingly. If so, the evangelists have resisted the temptation.

To set over against these points of difference I cannot find a single point of resemblance. If the theory of a displaced post-resurrection appearance is to be evoked for the understanding of this difficult *pericopé*, it must be without any support from form-criticism, and indeed in the teeth of the presumption which formal analysis establishes.

4. Some critics have proposed to interpret the story of the Stilling of the Storm in Mk. iv. 35–41 and parallels by a similar hypothesis, but once again the hypothesis finds no support in form-criticism. It might be held that, since the raging ocean out of all control is a symbol of primaeval chaos, and so of returning chaos at the end (cf. Lk. xxi. 25), and 'the voice of the Lord upon the waters' (Ps. xxix. 3) is a symbol of the divine sovereignty asserted over all rebellious powers, a scene in which Christ reduces the raging sea to submission by his word is a kind of '*parusia*'-scene; and if it be true (as Dr. Lightfoot has taught us, and as I believe) that Matt. xxviii. 16–20 is a kind of *parusia*-scene, it might be argued that the two scenes are in some sort equipollent. But it is precisely the apocalyptic imagery associated with the *parusia*-idea that is absent from Matt. xxviii and present (on this hypothesis) in the Storm-

pericopé. There is therefore no probability in the view that the Stilling of the Storm was in the original tradition a post-resurrection narrative. We may, however, reckon with the possibility that the tradition which underlies this *pericopé* had at some stage been influenced by apocalyptic conceptions, and had absorbed some of their imagery.

We have now exhausted all the passages in the gospels where the traditions regarding the appearance of Christ to his followers after his resurrection have been formed into narratives of the event, concise or circumstantial.[1] But there is another form in which such traditions were handed down, containing no such description of any single incident, but either offering a list of such incidents, or else summarizing the whole series in a comprehensive statement. We must now turn to passages of this kind.

Summaries and Lists

1. In Acts i. 3–4 we have a comprehensive summary of all that followed the resurrection of Christ. It runs as follows: 'He presented himself to the apostles alive after his Passion by means of many proofs,[2] appearing to them over a period of

---

[1] I have not included the story of the ascension, which is of a different character. In the 'Longer Ending' of Mark (xvi. 19) and the Received Text of Lk. xxiv. 51, it is scarcely more than an editorial winding-up of the series of incidents following the resurrection. In Acts i. 9–11 alone it is shaped into a real narrative, the main motive of which seems to be given in the concluding words of the angelic pronouncement.

[2] Ἐν πολλοῖς τεκμηρίοις: cf. Aristotle's category of recognition διὰ σημείων (proofs of identity) (*De Art. Poet.* 16.1454b.21). Aristotle might have said that Luke used the term loosely, since he elsewhere distinguishes τεκμήριον from σημεῖον (e.g. *Anal. Pr.* 27, especially p. 70b.2). But Luke perhaps knew what he was about: a τεκμήριον, in the Aristotelian use of terms, is a more *certain* kind of proof. Cf. Aeschylus, *Choeph.* 205: Orestes' footprints are δεύτερον τεκμήριον of the identity of the secret visitor to the tomb.

forty days, and speaking about the kingdom of God; and then, while he was eating with them (?),[1] he instructed them not to depart from Jerusalem but to await the promise of the Father. . . .' We are here at a wide remove from the living tradition. The summary is a literary composition by an author who looks back to what he has himself written in the first volume of his work (Lk. xxiv).

2. It is otherwise with the summary statements contained in the outline form of apostolic *kerygma* given in certain chapters of Acts. In chapters ii, iii, and v we are told no more than the bare fact that the apostles are witnesses to the resurrection of Christ. But the form of *kerygma* attributed to Peter in x. 34–43 is rather more explicit: 'God raised him up on the third day, and permitted him to become visible, not to all the people, but to witnesses previously chosen by God, namely to us, who ate and drank with him after he rose from the dead; and he instructed us to proclaim to the people. . . .' Similarly in the *kerygma* attributed to Paul in xiii. 16–41 we read, 'God raised him from the dead, and he appeared for several days to those who had accompanied him from Galilee to Jerusalem, and who are now his witnesses to the people'. (The change from 'us' to 'those who accompanied him' is dictated by the fact that this speech is assigned to Paul and not to any of the original apostles.)

If these forms of *kerygma* in Acts may be accepted as representing with reasonable fidelity the general type of early preaching, as I believe they may, then the gospel narratives which we have been examining would readily serve the purpose of exemplifying or illustrating the statements made in general terms in the *kerygma*. The 'concise' narratives would be precisely (in Dibelius's sense of the term) 'paradigms' for the use of the preacher.

3. In I Cor. xv. 3–8 we have something still more particular. After reporting the death, burial and resurrection of Christ, Paul adds a formal list of appearances of the risen Lord to various persons:

[1] The meaning of the word συναλιζόμενος is very uncertain. See Cadbury's excellent note *ad loc.*

'He appeared to Caphas,
    then to the Twelve.
After that he appeared to more than 500 brethren at once . . .
After that he appeared to James,
    then to all the apostles.
Last of all he appeared to me.'

This list of Christophanies Paul declares to form part of the *kerygma*, as it was set forth by all Christian missionaries of whatever rank or tendency (xv. 11), part of the 'tradition' which he had received (xv. 3), part of the 'Gospel' which the Corinthians had accepted when he evangelized Achaia (xv. 1). No statement could be more emphatic or unambiguous. In making it Paul is exposing himself to the criticism of resolute opponents, who would have been ready to point to any flaw in his credentials or in his presentation of the common tradition. Exactly how much of the list comes directly out of the common form of *kerygma* is not quite clear. The appearance to Paul himself is obviously not part of what he 'received'. The parenthetic remark that most of the 500 are still alive may well be an addition to the received formula, since it refers to a definite point of time—that, no doubt, at which the apostle was writing. The rest of the list, it appears, we must accept as part of the common and primitive tradition.[1]

We seem to have a further trace of the same formula in Lk. xxiv. 34. Luke intends here, as we have seen, to present a kind of comprehensive 'Gospel of the Resurrection' within the framework of a single narrative. In pursuance of this

---

[1] It has been suggested, and not without some plausibility, that the balanced statements, ὤφθη Κηφᾷ, εἶτα τοῖς δώδεκα· ὤφθη Ἰακώβῳ, εἶτα τοῖς ἀποστόλοις πᾶσιν, may derive from two separate lists, the one current in the tradition sponsored by Peter, the other in a tradition sponsored by James and the 'brothers' of Jesus (see note on p. 114). This is possible, but in that case we must certainly take it that the two lists had been combined before the formula was transmitted to Paul, since he expressly says that the list, as he gives it, was common to all Christian missionaries; and this was of controversial value to him, because it was representative of the party of James who were his principal opponents within the Church.

intention he makes 'the Eleven and those who were with them'
cap the remarkable news which Cleopas and his companion
have brought from Emmaus by announcing, 'The Lord has
indeed risen, and he appeared to Simon'. It is impossible to
miss the close parallel with I Cor. xv. 4–5.

Lk.   I Cor.

ὅτι ὄντως ἠγέρθη ὁ κύριος   ὅτι ἐγήγερται τῇ ἡμέρᾳ τῇ τρίτῃ[1]
καὶ ὤφθη Σίμωνι   καὶ ὅτι ὤφθη Κηφᾷ.

It is hardly doubtful that the evangelist was familiar with a
formula practically identical with that which Paul 'received'
and 'transmitted'. We should not miss the significance of the
fact that he is content to report the appearance to Peter in this
jejune kerygmatic form. However ready he may have been to
'write up' traditional material which had reached him, and
however great the skill he displays in doing so, he was clearly
not willing to create a whole story out of a bare statement like
this; otherwise, what a story we might have had of the appearance of Christ which was (to judge from various indications)
crucial for the whole history of the Church, but which has
inexplicably failed to enter into the gospels!

It is indeed a remarkable fact that the narratives in the
gospels are far from covering the whole ground of the list
given in the Pauline *kerygma*. We might regard Matt. xxviii.
16–20, Lk. xxiv. 36–43, Jn. xx. 19–21, Mk. xvi. 14–15, as
representing the appearances to 'the Twelve' and to 'all the
apostles', without being in a position to distinguish precisely
which is which. It has been suggested that Jn. xxi. represents
the appearance 'to Cephas', but it is certainly not an appearance
to Peter alone, perhaps not chiefly to Peter, since it is the
beloved disciple who first recognizes the Lord. The appearance
'to James' appears only in an apocryphal gospel. That the
appearance 'to above 500 brethren at once' may be represented

---

[1] The Lucan form naturally does not include 'the third day', for
ex hypothesi it is on 'the third day' that the words are spoken; the
reader already knows that from the very emphatic statement xxiv.
21; σὺν πᾶσιν τούτοις τρίτην ταύτην ἡμέραν ἄγει.

by the account of Pentecost in Acts ii, the descent of the Spirit being a surrogate for the presence of the Lord (perhaps in the sense of Jn. xiv. 16–19, or even of II Cor. iii. 17), was a suggestion which at one time commanded some favour, but it remains a pure speculation.

It appears, then, that the narratives in the gospels were not produced as expansion, by way of commentary or 'midrash', of the list of appearances in the primitive tradition; while it is quite certain that the list was not compiled out of the gospels. We must conclude that the list of successive appearances on the one hand, as we have it in I Cor. xv. 3–8, and as it is implied in Lk. xxiv. 33–4, and on the other hand the different types of narrative in the gospels, are independent of one another, and represent alternative methods of supplementing the simple statements of the *kerygma* in its baldest form, that Christ rose from the dead and that the apostles were witnesses to the fact, since he appeared to them after his Passion.

The motives underlying the two different methods may perhaps be distinguished by examining the forms. In the gospel narratives of Class I, which, we have reason to suppose, represent most closely the corporate oral tradition of the primitive Church, the witnesses are usually the apostolic body as a whole (whether identified as 'the Eleven', or 'the Eleven and those with them', or in other ways). Names of individuals are not mentioned. An apparent exception is Matt. xxviii. 9–10, where, in view of xxviii. 1, the reader identifies the women as Mary Magdalen and 'the other Mary' (whoever she may have been). But if we were right in isolating xxviii. 9–10 as an independent *pericopé*, the individual names may not have been present originally. In any case, the intention in general seems to be to present the facts as attested corporately by the apostolic body (using that term in the widest sense), in the spirit of I Jn. i. 1–3. Credence is invited, not on the testimony of a given witness, but on the authority of the apostolic tradition embodied in the Church. Where we have apologetic expansions of the narrative, they are directed towards meeting the objection that the apostles themselves may have had insufficient grounds for making the claims they do make. Various τεκμήρια are adduced, but these still rest upon the corporate testimony of the apostolic body. In the end it all goes back to the affirmation of that authoritative group, who say, in answer to questions raised, 'That which we have seen, that which we have heard with our ears and our hands have handled, we declare to you'. Either their word is to be accepted, upon the whole matter, or there is nothing further to be done.

In the formula of I Cor. xv. 3–8, on the contrary, there seems to be an attempt to meet a possible objector to some extent by defining more precisely the source of information, so as to put him (in theory at least) in a position to question the witness. There can hardly be any purpose in mentioning the fact that most of the 500 are still alive, unless Paul is saying, in effect, 'the witnesses are there to be questioned'. And it is not the same thing to appeal to the authority of 'the Eleven and those with them' or the like, and to mention Cephas and James as individuals. Cephas was well-known to the Corinthians, whether directly or not; James was a name to conjure with among many who belittled Paul himself. Certainly Paul appeals to the consensus of all Christian missionaries: this is the same appeal to a generalized apostolic authority that underlies the forms of 'concise' narrative in the gospels. But it is of advantage to him that he can adduce an agreed statement which particularizes the authorities.

In the 'circumstantial' narratives of the gospels also individual names are introduced; but the motive here is the enrichment of the story rather than the strengthening of the evidence. The introduction of names into a story which was originally anonymous is noted by the form-critics in general as a feature of 'legend'. It by no means follows that the names are unhistorical, but it is probably true, here as in analogous cases, that the main reason why the names are given is that they lend greater interest and vividness to the narrative. To recognize this is to underline the entirely different purpose of the mention of names in the *kerygmatic* formula of I Cor. xv.

4. There is one more passage which should be placed alongside Paul's list for comparison—the 'Longer Ending' of Mark, part of which we have already considered. Mk. xvi. 14–15 seemed on examination to be a fairly typical example of a 'concise' narrative based upon the common oral tradition. Yet

it appears here as the climax of what looks like a list not altogether dissimilar from that of I Cor. xv:

> ' He appeared first to Mary Magdalen . . .
>
> After this he appeared to two of them as they were journeying into the country . . .
>
> Later, he appeared to the Eleven themselves as they sat at table. . . .

The sequence, πρῶτον . . . μετὰ δὲ ταῦτα . . . ὕστερον, recalls the εἶτα . . . ἔπειτα . . . ἔπειτα . . . εἶτα . . . ἔσχατον πάντων of I Cor. xv. 3–8. We must therefore examine the passage more closely.

If this was a list analogous to that of I Cor. xv, it must have had a rather fuller form, since in each case we are told something more than the bare fact that the Lord appeared to such-and-such a person. But apart from that, the list does not seem calculated to serve the precise purpose which we inferred to have been in view in the construction of the Pauline list. The latter, as we saw, reinforces the statements of the *kerygma* by particularizing the sources of evidence, especially by singling out the great names of Peter and James. In Mk. xvi. the appearance to 'the Eleven' may be taken to represent what I have called the generalized authority of apostolic tradition. It goes no further. The appearance to two unidentified persons on a journey to some unnamed place adds nothing to the evidence, for the purpose in view. Only Mary Magdalen is specified by name. It is doubtful whether for the wider public her name would carry much weight. Indeed the writer himself goes on to say that 'those who had been with him' did not believe a word she said. There would seem to have been some reluctance on the part of the Church, or its spokesmen, to place much weight upon her evidence. That is perhaps why her name does not figure in the official list adopted, as Paul declares, by all Christian missionaries. It does not appear, then, that the list in Mk. xvi was shaped by the same motives as that given by Paul.

Then should we conclude that the appearances to Mary Magdalen in xvi. 9–11 and to the two companions in 12–13 are, like the appearance to the Eleven in xvi. 14–15, forms of 'concise' narrative in a highly concentrated form (though scarcely more concentrated than Matt. xxviii. 9–10)? Against

that view there are the following considerations: (*a*) the narratives, though extremely brief, contain details not essential to
the main theme, similar in character to those which appear in
the 'circumstantial' narratives: the description of Mary Magdalen as one 'out of whom he had cast seven devils'; the Eleven
'lamenting and weeping' (an unparalleled trait); the appearance
of the Lord 'in another form'; (*b*) the longest and most emphatic parts of these little stories are those which describe,
not the appearance of the Lord itself, nor the recognition of
him by his followers, but the reporting of the incident to
others and its unfavourable reception (xvi. 10–11, 13). There
is therefore no such specific formative motive at work as we
can recognize elsewhere. It is only when we look at the list
as a whole that a possible guiding idea may be discerned.
The whole stress is laid upon the appearance to the Eleven,
which serves to introduce the Lord's command to his Church
(which in some MSS. is greatly expanded), his ascension, and
the summary of the early Christian mission which concludes
the passage. The two incidents briefly touched upon in xvi.
9–13 serve only to introduce the main incident, and to exhibit
the unbelief with which the reports of Mary Magdalen and
the two companions are received, as a foil to the faith of the
Church. The contrast of belief and unbelief is in fact a prominent theme of xvi. 14–20.

While we saw no definite reason to conclude that the
narrative in xvi. 14–15 was derived from any of our canonical
gospels, it does appear that verses 9–13 may be derivative.
Mary Magdalen 'out of whom he had cast seven devils', is
almost verbally after Lk. viii. 2. The reception of her report
recalls the statement of Lk. xxiv. 11 that the report which she
and other women brought about the empty Tomb was similarly received: 'They thought they were talking nonsense, and
disbelieved them' (ἠπίστουν αὐταῖς in Lk., ἠπίστησαν in Mk.).
With these echoes in mind, we shall be disposed to think that
the appearance to the two companions came out of Lk. xxiv.
rather than directly out of oral tradition. The appearance to
Mary Magdalen however cannot itself have come from Luke.
It may have been derived from John or from Matthew (by
singling out one of the two women of whom Matthew speaks).

The 'Longer Ending' does not otherwise show any clear mark of dependence on John, while the command to go and preach to all the world, and the institution of baptism (xvi. 15–16), resemble Matt. xxviii. 19 fairly closely. The record of the ascension, on the other hand (xvi. 19), being entirely in biblical language (II Kings ii. 11 LXX + Ps. cx. 1), does not appear to depend on Acts i. 9.

The most probable conclusion seems to be that the author of the 'Longer Ending' is in the main composing freely out of current tradition, but drawing upon Matthew and Luke for part of his material.[1] As a summary of what happened after the discovery of the empty Tomb it carries no independent authority.

We may now summarize the conclusions to which the investigation seems to have led, and draw some corollaries.

1. The earliest extant form in which the appearances of the risen Lord are reported is an ordered list of such appearances to specified individuals and groups, which was included in the *kerygma* of the early Church as it was communicated to Paul. Its purpose seems to have been to provide interested enquirers with a guaranteed statement of the sources of evidence upon which the affirmations of the *kerygma* were grounded.

2. Perhaps equally early in origin, though transmitted to us in a later document, are the bare statements contained in other forms of the *kerygma*, to the effect that the apostles are witnesses to the resurrection, inasmuch as Christ appeared to them alive after death. Here there is no attempt to deploy the sources of evidence: the statement is made, like the *kerygma* as a whole, upon the collective authority of the apostolic body.

3. In the gospels there is a series of concise *pericopae*, bearing the marks of a corporate oral tradition, in which the appearances

[1] For another example of the combination of material drawn from a canonical gospel with an independent rendering of oral tradition I should wish to refer to the fragment of an unknown gospel in Egerton Papyrus 2, the composition of which may well be nearly contemporary with that of the 'Longer Ending' of Mark; see my argument in the *Bulletin of the John Rylands Library*, vol. 20, no. 1, Jan. 1936, reprinted in *New Testament Studies* (M.U.P.), pp. 12–52. But not all critics take that view of **Eg. Pap. 2.**

of Christ to individuals and groups are briefly described. The points upon which emphasis is laid are (*a*) the recognition of the Lord by his disciples, almost always with the implication that such recognition was neither immediate nor inevitable; and (*b*) the word of command given by Christ to his followers. These two elements are apt to be expanded in more-developed examples of this type of *pericopé*, (*a*) by the tender of proofs of the reality of the Person who appeared, and of his identity with the Crucified, and (*b*) by the introduction of further material appropriate as a final charge to the apostles. These *pericopae* do not mention individual names. They put forward their statements, like the forms of *kerygma* under 2, upon the collective authority of the apostolic body, and may well have served as 'paradigms' or illustrative examples for preachers. They show no sign of having been derived from the authorized list of appearances under 1. Their formative idea we may take to be: The Christ who died is the living Guide and Ruler of his Church; Matthew adds, the Lord of heaven and earth.

4. There are other *pericopae* in the gospels which give a more circumstantial narrative of the appearances. The added matter is almost entirely of the nature of dramatic or picturesque detail, especially in the presentation of the recognition of the Lord by his disciples. A marked feature is the introduction of a common meal at which the risen Lord 'breaks bread' for his disciples. The resurrection is thus associated with the eucharistic ideas and practice of the early Church. For the rest, it cannot be said that these circumstantial narratives alter the perspective or the implications of the briefer type of narrative.

5. Negatively, the gospel narratives, of whatever type, are entirely free from the conventional apparatus of apocalypse. There are no supernatural signs accompanying the appearances,[1] and the risen Christ communicates no revelations of

---

[1] It is, of course, true that the risen Christ is visible or invisible at will, and that closed doors are no bar to his entrance. This feature is a necessary *datum* of the situation, and though it is, no doubt, abnormal or praeternatural, it has little in common with the stuff of apocalyptic visions. With the narrative of the ascension we pass into the sphere of apocalypse.

the secrets of the other world, as he is often made to do in later apocryphal works. Even though in Matthew Christ appears as Lord of heaven and earth, his lordship is not signified by any kind of portent: his word is sufficient.

It has been not unusual to apply the term 'myth' somewhat loosely to the resurrection-narratives of the gospels as a whole. The foregoing investigation will have shown that, so far as the narratives of the appearances of the risen Christ are concerned, form-criticism offers no ground to justify the use of the term. The more circumstantial narratives certainly include traits properly described as legendary,[1] but 'legend' and 'myth' are different categories, and should not be confused. *Formally*, there is nothing to distinguish the narratives we have been examining from the 'Paradigms' and other concise narratives on the one hand, and the '*Novellen*', or 'Tales', on the other, which occur in other parts of the gospels, and they merit the same degree of critical consideration, not only in their aspect as witnesses to the faith of the early Church, but also as ostensible records of things that happened.

[1] The term 'legend', as a formal category, does not carry any necessary judgement about the factual truth of the story. It refers to a manner of telling the story. The relation of legend to fact is different from that of (let us say) a chronicle or a letter from someone concerned, but the relation exists, and should be investigated.

9 Ἔννομος Χριστοῦ

In I Corinthians ix. 19–22 Paul states, in a series of balanced or antithetical clauses, several ways in which he voluntarily restricts his personal liberty in the interests of his missionary endeavours.

The general principle is that he adapts his behaviour (in things indifferent, *bien entendu*) to the circle to which he desires at the moment to appeal: τοῖς πᾶσιν γέγονα πάντα ἵνα πάντως τινὰς σώσω. Thus, in appealing to persons who are 'weak' (by which we are to understand scrupulous, in Paul's opinion morbidly scrupulous), he is ready to behave 'as weak'; that is to say, as if he shared their morbid scruples, from which in fact he is free. His meaning is clear from the example given in the foregoing chapter. If he is in the company of a fellow-Christian who has scruples about eating certain foods, he will himself abstain, in contrast to those who, boasting of their 'strong-mindedness', will insist on partaking of food which in their judgment is entirely harmless, without regard to the scruples of their company (viii. 9–13). In the present passage the persons in view are probably not scrupulous Christians, since they are persons whom Paul wished to 'win';[1] we may take them to be non-Christians, presumably of Jewish religion, who cherish similar scruples. So far, so good.

We now turn to the other examples given of the same principle of adaptability in missionary practice. 'To the Jews', Paul writes, 'I made myself like a Jew, to win Jews.' But by birth, nationality and upbringing Paul *was* a Jew: how could he say that he became *like* a Jew? To clear up that point he repeats, 'To those who are under the law I behaved as if under the law, though I am myself not under the law.' That removes any possibility of misunderstanding or ambiguity: in one sense, it is true, Paul is a Jew, but not in the sense of one who submits to the authority of the law of Moses; in that sense he is

---

[1] Yet in Matt. xviii. 15 (a passage which, as we shall see, has some obscure relation to certain passages in Paul) κερδαίνειν is used of winning back an erring brother.

not a Jew, but behaves *as if* he were a Jew, that is, as if he were subject to the Mosaic law. Thus the meaning of νόμος in verse 20 is plain: it is the Torah, as written in the Pentateuch and expounded by orthodox Jewish rabbis. When Paul is endeavouring to convert Jews, he means, he voluntarily submits to the precepts and prohibitions of the Torah, although as a Christian he holds himself to be free from them.

In the light of this we approach the next clause: 'to the lawless, I behaved as if lawless'. Clearly, as οἱ ὑπὸ νόμον is equivalent to οἱ Ἰουδαῖοι, so οἱ ἄνομοι is equivalent, in Paul's intention', to 'Gentiles'.[1] When he is out to win Gentiles to Christianity, he, though a born Jew, will behave as if he were himself a Gentile to whom the Mosaic law meant nothing. As a Christian he did in fact consider himself to be as free from the obligations of the Torah as any Gentile, though for different reasons. It occurs to him, however, as he writes (or dictates), that the expression ἄνομος might very well be gravely misunderstood by readers to whom the equivalence of νόμος and Torah was by no means familiar. He must guard his statement carefully against such misunderstanding. Although he behaves ὡς ἄνομος, he is not ἄνομος, in the sense of leading an unregulated and irresponsible life:[2] τοῖς ἀνόμοις ὡς ἄνομος (ἐγενόμην), μὴ ὢν ἄνομος. That would seem to be clear enough. And yet, in the sense in which he has used the term νόμος in the preceding sentence he *is* ἄνομος, μὴ ὢν αὐτὸς ὑπὸ νόμον. Evidently some further clarification is required.

He therefore qualifies ἄνομος by the addition of Θεοῦ. Although he is not subject to the Torah, or law of Moses, yet he is not 'without the law of God'. It is evident that (in this place at least) the Torah is not conceived as being identical,

---

[1] The special *nuance* of ἄνομος in the mouth of a Jew is well illustrated by Acts ii. 23: it is a part of the gravamen of the charge against the Jews who brought Christ to his death that they made use of heathen Romans to do their dirty work.

[2] In I Tim. i. 9 ἄνομος clearly has the wider sense of 'uncontrolled by any law'. It is equated with ἀνυπότακτος and explicated in a typical list of heathen vices and crimes. It is the epithet ἄνομος in this sense that Paul is anxious to disavow.

or equivalent, or at any rate co-extensive, with the law of God,
which is either a different, or a more inclusive, law than the
law of Moses.

Elsewhere in the Pauline epistles the expression, 'the law of
God', is found only in a single context, Romans vii. 7–viii. 10.
All through that discussion the sense to be attached to νόμος
in any particular place is notoriously elusive. In vii. 7 ὁ νόμος
(without qualification) is clearly the Torah, since it is exempli-
fied by the tenth commandment of the Decalogue. But we read
also of ὁ νόμος τοῦ νοός μου, ὁ νόμος τοῦ πνεύματος τῆς ζωῆς,
as well as (ὁ) νόμος (τοῦ) Θεοῦ, and how precisely these terms
are to be related to one another is not entirely clear. Over
against the law of God, again, is a ἕτερος νόμος which enslaves
a man to a 'law of sin', otherwise called ὁ νόμος τῆς ἁμαρτίας
καὶ τοῦ θανάτου. In these expressions once again the sense to
be given to νόμος is not entirely clear.[1] Without purporting
to discuss, still less to settle, problems which have been the

---

[1] Is the ἕτερος νόμος of vii. 23 to be distinguished from the 'law
of sin' to which it enslaves a man? If so, is the 'law of sin and death'
to be identified with the commandments of the Torah which, finding
an ἀφορμή in sin, lead to death? Or is the ἕτερος νόμος, in spite of the
form of the sentence, identical with the νόμος ἁμαρτίας and is the
latter conceived as a kind of anti-Torah—the Decalogue with all
the negatives left out, shall we say? Or is the ἕτερος νόμος a 'law' in the
non-Hebraic sense of 'regulative principle' (as we speak of 'laws of
nature'), and is this 'law' which fights against the νόμος τοῦ νοός no
other than the יצר הרע striving against the יצר הטוב, only given a
Greek dress? If this Greek sense of the word can be accepted, then
the expression εὑρίσκω τὸν νόμον in vii. 21 can be understood quite
simply: 'I discover this principle', viz. the principle otherwise
expressed in the maxim, 'video meliora proboque, deteriora sequor',
and there is no need to assume an awkward ellipse or anacoluthon,
or an intolerably harsh use of the 'accusative of respect'. It is difficult to avoid the impression that in this discussion Paul is playing
(consciously or not) upon various meanings of a Greek term of
wide connotation, while he is yet haunted by the conventional equivalence, for a Jew, of νόμος and Torah. See what I have written in
The Bible and the Greeks (Hodder and Stoughton, 1935), pp. 25–41.

daily meat of controversialists for centuries, I would suggest
that the various forms of expression would be consistent with
a conception of the 'law of God' as something wider and more
inclusive than the 'law' *simpliciter*, in the sense of Torah. At
one stage and on one level this law of God is represented by
the Torah, and on that level a man's response to the Torah is,
quite genuinely, a response to the law of God; as a man who
disobeys the precept μή ἐπιθυμήσῃς is disobeying the law of
God. At another stage and upon a different level the law of
God may be mediated in some other, perhaps some more
adequate form, in which it may be obeyed by one who is not
longer subject to Torah. A similar sense for νόμος Θεοῦ would
suit the expression μὴ ἄνομος Θεοῦ in I Cor. ix. 21.

Upon this basis we might understand what Paul means when
he goes on to say that he is ἔννομος Χριστοῦ, an expression
which implies the existence of a νόμος Χριστοῦ. The law of
God, which at one stage and on one level finds expression in
the Torah, may at another stage and on a different level find
expression in the 'law of Christ'.

We may then read the implied debate between Paul and his
opponents which underlies I Cor. ix. 20-1 somewhat as
follows: Paul declares that he is not ὑπὸ νόμον, meaning, not
subject to Torah. His Jewish adversary counters, 'Then you
are, by your own confession, ἄνομος, a lawless, ungovernable,
dissolute heathen.' 'No,' Paul retorts, 'you are assuming an
unwarranted identity of the Torah with the ultimate law of
God. A man may be free from Torah and yet be loyal to the law
of God, as it is represented or expressed in the law of Christ.
Being myself subject to the law of Christ, I am no stranger
to the law of God, although I claim freedom from the Torah.'

We have now to ask, how is this 'law of Christ' to be conceived? What is its character, in what form is it apprehended
by men, and how is it obeyed? The actual expression, 'law of
Christ', it is true, is only *implied* in our present passage, but
it occurs explicitly in one other passage of the Pauline epistles
(and only one)—Galatians vi. 2: οὕτως ἀναπληρώσατε (v.l.
ἀναπληρώσετε) τὸν νόμον τοῦ Χριστοῦ. Whether we read the
imperative of the verb, or the future in a 'promissory apodosis',
the meaning, for our purpose, does not greatly differ. The

K

phrase is embedded in a series of moral injunctions forming part of what is called the 'ethical section' of the epistle. The implication is that in obeying these injunctions—or, less probably, in obeying the one which immediately precedes ('Bear one another's burdens')—a man will be fulfilling the law of Christ; or, in other words, in acknowledging himself bound by such injunctions he is ἔννομος Χριστοῦ. To this extent at least, it would seem, the law of Christ is such that it can be stated in the form of a code of precepts to which a Christian man is obliged to conform.

The whole series of precepts, however, is introduced (in v. 16) by the general maxim, πνεύματι περιπατεῖτε, which is virtually repeated in πνεύματι ἄγεσθε (18), πνεύματι στοιχῶμεν (25). In 22-3 the virtues of Christian living are described as 'fruit of the Spirit', rather than as obedience to precepts. The 'Spirit', over against the 'flesh', is represented as an immanent power in men making for such virtues as charity, patience, gentleness and self-control. If in this sense a man is 'led by the Spirit', he is not ὑπὸ νόμον (v. 18). And yet, in exhibiting the 'spirit of gentleness' in human relations he is also 'fulfilling the law of Christ' (vi. 1-2). The concept of the Spirit here appears as a kind of background to the same subtle distinction as we found to be drawn in I Cor. ix. 20. There, Paul described himself as μὴ ὢν ὑπὸ νόμον, and yet as ἔννομος Χριστοῦ, and so here the Christian, in so far as he is led by the Spirit, is οὐχ ὑπὸ νόμον and yet he is said to 'fulfil the law of Christ'.

It is a further complication of the thought that the exercise of ἀγάπη, which in v. 22 is the primary 'fruit of the Spirit', is in v. 14 the fulfilment of the precept ἀγαπήσεις τὸν πλησίον σου ὡς σεαυτόν, which is a commandment of the Torah. We may, however, ask what is Paul's authority for the statement that in the precept of love to neighbour ὁ πᾶς νόμος πεπλήρωται. There seems to be evidence for suggestions to this effect among rabbis of the school of Hillel, but there is certainly a quite explicit statement, handed down in the tradition of the sayings of Jesus which came to be embodied in the gospels.[1] It would perhaps not be going too far if we said that the

[1] In the gospels, of course, the sum of the law consists of *two*

ultimate law of God can be discerned in the Torah when it is interpreted by Christ; and this may help to clarify the relation between the fluctuating conceptions of νόμος in I Cor. ix. 20–1.

How then is obedience to the law of Christ, which is also obedience to the law of God embodied in the Torah when it is rightly valued and understood, related to the concept diversely expressed in the terms πνεύματι ἄγεσθαι, στοιχεῖν, περιπατεῖν? Are we to say that the law of Christ is no other than what is elsewhere described as the 'law of the Spirit', and is this the law which is οὐ γράμματος ἀλλὰ πνεύματος (II Cor. iii. 6)? And does this mean that the law of Christ is incapable of being written down 'in black and white', or inscribed on stone, like the Decalogue (and the decrees of Greek city-states)? Is it known solely by inner promptings of the Spirit?

At this point we must be careful about the use of Pauline phraseology. The expression 'law of the Spirit'—just so—does not in fact occur. In Romans viii. 2 we read, ὁ νόμος τοῦ πνεύματος τῆς ζωῆς ἐν Χριστῷ Ἰησοῦ ἠλευθέρωσέν σε. Paul's easygoing ways with Greek syntax make it difficult to say precisely how he intended this to be construed. But the connection of πνεῦμα with ζωή recalls Gal. v. 25, πνεύματι ζῶμεν. Here to 'live by the Spirit' is the way to liberty; similarly in Romans, loc. cit., the 'law of the Spirit of life' has set men free; cf. also II Cor. iii. 17. In Galatians such liberty is the condition under which Christians are to 'serve one another in love' (Gal. v. 13), or, in other words, to 'fulfil the law of Christ' (Gal. vi. 2). This is to 'walk by the Spirit', and 'walking by the Spirit' is distinguishable from 'living by the Spirit'. The two are not simply identical; the former is the consequence of the latter (Gal. v. 25). By analogy, it is likely that the 'law

---

commandments; but there is no real contradiction. In so far as the law of God is directed towards ethical behaviour in human relations, it is summed up in the single command to love one's neighbour as oneself. There is a certain parallel between Matthew's ἐν ταύταις ταῖς δυσὶν ἐντολαῖς ὅλος ὁ νόμος κρέμαται and Paul's ὁ πᾶς νόμος ἐν ἑνὶ λόγῳ πεπλήρωται. The parallel is perhaps not without significance, in view of some curious apparent contacts between Paul and the tradition of the Sayings in Matthew. See below.

of the Spirit of life'[1] in Romans is conceived as the regulative
principle bringing about the condition of liberty under which
it is possible to 'walk by the Spirit', or, to use the expression
common to Romans and Galatians, to be 'led by the Spirit'
(Rom. viii. 14, Gal. v. 18). Hence it is unlikely that the expression ὁ νόμος τοῦ πνεύματος connotes a 'law' in the sense of
a code of precepts dictated by the inner prompting of the Spirit
instead of by a written document of any kind. The term νόμος
therefore would seem to be used here in a sense in which it
does not correspond to 'Torah', but approximates rather to
its Greek use in the sense of a regulative principle; and this
view is supported by the occurrence of the term ὁ νόμος τοῦ
νοός in the immediate context, since the concepts πνεῦμα and
νοῦς lie fairly close together in early Christian thought, as in
that of Hellenistic Judaism.[2] Thus the expression ὁ νόμος τοῦ
πνεύματος must not be taken as parallel to the expression
ὁ νόμος τοῦ Χριστοῦ.[3] We might put it thus: ὁ νόμος τοῦ
πνεύματος τῆς ζωῆς corresponds to πνεύματι ζῶμεν and ὁ
νόμος τοῦ Χριστοῦ corresponds to πνεύματι στοιχῶμεν. It follows
that we are not obliged, by the emphasis laid upon the doctrine
of the Spirit in the immediate context, to interpret the νόμος
τοῦ Χριστοῦ of Gal. vi. 2 in a sense which excludes the *prima
facie* suggestion of a 'law' in some sort analogous to the Torah.

We therefore enquire afresh whether there is any positive
evidence that Paul did in fact so conceive the Law of Christ,

[1] Are we to understand 'the law of the life-giving Spirit', or 'the
spiritual law of life'? And is ἐν Χριστῷ Ἰησοῦ to be joined with ζωῆς
(*qs.* τῆς ἐν Χριστῷ Ἰησοῦ) or with ἠλευθέρωσεν? These are only
some of the ambiguities involved.

[2] A striking example in Paul is the sudden intrusion of νοῦς into a
context which has been concerned with πνεῦμα in I Cor. ii. 15–16.
It is true that this is conditioned by the language of the LXX of
Isaiah to which Paul is referring, but that fact serves only to underline the ease with which Hellenistic Judaism passed from the one
concept to the other. See my book, *The Interpretation of the Fourth
Gospel* (Cambridge University Press, 1953), pp. 213–37.

[3] I withdraw here the view I expressed, without sufficient consideration, in *The Bible and the Greeks*, p. 37.

and for this purpose we turn back in the first place to the epistle from which our fundamental text was taken. It happens that in the same epistle, and at points not far removed from the text from which we started, he has occasion to refer to certain maxims belonging to the tradition of the teaching of Jesus. In I Cor. ix. 14 he cites an 'ordinance' of Christ to the effect that Christian preachers are entitled to maintenance: ὁ Κύριος διέταξεν in his formula. The verb διατάσσειν, meaning primarily to 'arrange', 'dispose', was used at this period of the issue of a decree or edict by the competent authority. Διάταγμα is a technical term for the edict of the Emperor or his representative.[1] Similarly in the New Testament the verb and the noun are used (e.g.) of a decree of the Emperor Claudius (Acts xviii. 2), of military orders (Acts xxiii. 31, xxiv. 23, Lk. iii. 13) and of a command of God to Moses which was embodied in the Torah (Acts vii. 44). Such uses must be borne in mind when we find διατάσσειν used with Christ as subject, as in I Cor. ix. 14, and in Matt. xi. 1, where Jesus gives instructions, which amount to commands, to the Twelve in dispatching them on their mission. It is, in fact, in this last context that we find the substance of the διάταγμα which Paul here adduces. It seems therefore clear that his intention is to clinch his argument by appealing to a positive precept of Christ; and if the verb διατάσσειν does not in itself necessarily connote a strictly legislative enactment, it is clear that a διάταγμα is a proper constituent of law, as the Emperor's edict was in fact one of the main constituents of the corpus of Roman Law. If therefore, a few verses later, Paul speaks (by implication) of the 'law of Christ', it would be unnatural to deny that he regarded such a positive precept as that of Matt. x. 10 as an element in that law.[2]

[1] See the evidence in Moulton and Milligan, *Vocabulary of the Greek Testament*, s.v.

[2] In I Cor. vii. 17, xi. 34, xvi. 1, Paul uses διατάσσειν of the instructions which he himself gives to the churches of his foundation. Here the verb may be held to retain its older and weaker sense. It is not a διάταγμα as such, but the διάταγμα *of Christ*, as it is the διάταγμα of Caesar, that carries the authority of law. Yet as Caesar's

In I Cor. vii a different term is used for the precepts of Christ: ἐπιταγή (vii. 25); for in denying that there is any ἐπιταγή of the Lord περὶ παρθένων Paul clearly implies that the precept which he has cited (vii. 10) upon the indissolubility of marriage *is* an ἐπιταγὴ Κυρίου, although there he has used the more colourless term παραγγέλλειν.[1] Ἐπιτάσσειν has perhaps from the outset a more authoritarian tone than διατάσσειν, and in the LXX it is used several times to translate צוה, whence מצוה, one of the three main constituents of Hebrew law.[2] Paul therefore would appear to agree with the evangelists in regarding the precept γυναῖκα ἀπὸ ἀνδρὸς μὴ χωρισθῆναι, . . . καὶ ἄνδρα γυναῖκα μὴ ἀφιέναι as a legislative act of Christ. More strictly, they regard it as an authoritative interpretation of the aboriginal law of man's creation, or, as Paul might have put it, of the 'law of God', as distinct from the law of Moses (from which it is in fact expressly distinguished in Mk. x. 3–9, Matt. xix. 4–9). As such, Paul contrasts the ἐπιταγή of Christ with his own γνώμη, even though he believes that γνώμη to be directed by the Spirit (vii. 25, 40). He would no doubt have claimed that his gloss upon the precept of indissoluble marriage (vii. 11a) was similarly directed. Yet it appears that the actual ἐπιταγὴ Κυρίου remains uniquely authoritative.[3]

---

representatives in the provinces may issue a διάταγμα which may have the virtual force of law, so the Lord has delegated to his apostle authority for the building up of the Church, and is in virtue of this authority that he issues his διατάγματα (II Cor. xiii. 10).

[1] It is used, e.g., of a summons to appear before the court, and of army orders.

[2] מצות חקים ומשפטים Deut. viii. 11 *et passim*. See *The Bible and the Greeks*. pp. 25–30.

[3] According to some of our textual authorities we have in I Cor. xiv. 37 yet another term of legal colour: Κυρίου ἐντολή. Ἐντολή is in the LXX the normal rendering of מצוה, and in the New Testament it is the accepted term for a single 'commandment' out of the Torah, though it is also used occasionally of commands issued by (e.g.) Jewish or Christian ecclesiastical authorities. Apart from the present passage it is apparently only in the Johannine writings that ἐντολή is used of a 'commandment' of Christ (or, it may be, collectively of

The precepts which are cited in I Cor. vii. 10–11, ix. 14, are the only such precepts in the Pauline epistles expressly attributed to 'the Lord'. Yet there are numerous places where it is difficult not to recognize an unavowed reference to sayings

---

his commandments as a whole). The difficulty in I Cor. xiv. 37 is to find in the context any maxim which has the specific, pointed, self-contained form which is characteristic of an *ἐντολή*: *ἅ γράφω ὑμῖν* is vague enough, and might cover anything in ch. xiv, or indeed in the whole discussion of *πνευματικά* in chs. viii–xiv. There is indeed in xiv. 34 an allusion to what might well be called an *ἐντολή*, but that is said to be from the 'law', which in such a connection must surely mean the Torah (presumably Gen. iii. 16), and to suppose that *Κυρίου ἐντολή* in xiv. 37 means 'a commandment of Jahweh' would be out of harmony with Pauline usage. If we go farther back, it is no doubt possible to isolate sentences which have in some measure the form of *ἐντολαί*, but there is nothing which connects itself either in form or content with the type of dominical saying with which we are familiar from other sources. Some MSS. and versions read the plural *ἐντολαί*, and even if the singular is read, it would seem almost necessary to understand it as collective, virtually = 'law' as a sum of individual commandments (as possibly in Jn. xii. 50, II Pet. ii. 21, iii. 2). But the word *ἐντολή* is not present in D*FG Origen. It might conceivably have been supplied by a scribe or editor who felt some difficulty in the genitive *Κυρίου* as predicate. The words *ἅ γράφω ὑμῖν Κυρίου ἐστίν* might readily be understood to mean, 'All that I here write to you is dominical', the sense being that although Paul can adduce no *διάταγμα* or *ἐπιταγή Κυρίου* upon these disputed matters, yet his teaching has upon it the stamp of Christ. It is 'Christian' teaching in the strictest sense, and this Christian character will be discerned in it by the *προφήτης ἤ πνευματικός*: if not, the less prophet he! If this interpretation be adopted, we should probably understand that Paul would equally have said of his teaching about 'virgins' in vii. 25 sqq., *Κυρίου ἐστίν*, even though he could not cite an *ἐπιταγή Κυρίου*. In any case, while he might well have regarded that *ἐπιταγή Κυρίου* about marriage, and his *διάταγμα* about the maintenance of preachers, as entering into a 'law' of Christ, it is by no means so clear that he would so have regarded his own injunctions in this section of the epistle.

which form part of the tradition of the teaching of Jesus embodied in the gospels. Especially significant are the repeated echoes in the course of the discussion in Rom. xiv. There may be said to be here two main lines of argument. In verses 1–9 Paul argues in the main from first principles, drawn ultimately from the fundamental affirmation of the Gospel, that Christ died and rose again to become Lord of all (7–9). The second line of argument (verses 10–23) proceeds in the main not from first principles but from certain general ethical maxims which the writer assumes, and which he expects his readers to accept. Thus, it is to be assumed that 'all things are clean' and that 'nothing is unclean of itself' (20, 14). To many of Paul's readers that would be far from self-evident, yet his argument falls to the ground if he cannot assume its truth. On what grounds, then, does he affirm this maxim? Πέπεισμαι ἐν Κυρίῳ ᾿Ιησοῦ, he says. In itself that might mean no more than 'I am convinced in virtue of my union with Christ as a member of his body', which would certainly have been intended if he had written ἐν Κυρίῳ simply, or ἐν Χριστῷ; but if it means no more than that, it is not easy to see what reply Paul would have to one who should say 'and *I* am convinced in the Lord that the reverse is true'. The use of the form Κύριος ᾿Ιησοῦς, however, suggests the intention of referring to the historic Person, as in I Thess. ii. 15, I Cor. xi. 23. Cf. p. 25 above. It is therefore significant that among the sayings of Jesus in the gospels we read the maxim, οὐδέν ἐστιν ἔξωθεν τοῦ ἀνθρώπου εἰσπορευόμενον εἰς αὐτὸν ὃ δύναται κοινῶσαι αὐτόν, to which is appended the note, καθαρίζων πάντα τὰ βρώματα (Mk. vii. 18–19).[1] Again, the rhetorical question, τί κρίνεις τὸν ἀδελφόν σου, with the reminder of coming judgment, gains force if it is intended to recall the saying, μὴ κρίνετε . . . ἐν ᾧ γὰρ κρίματι κρίνετε κριθήσεσθε (Matt. vii. 1–2). The associated question,

---

[1] The participle in the masculine is the best attested reading, to be construed with the subject of λέγει in verse 18. Καθαρίζον, καθαρίζει, καθαρίζεται, all implying an alternative way of understanding the sentence, have inferior authority. Note that κοινός, κοινοῦν, in this sense are not elsewhere used by Paul, and are exclusively biblical (3 or 4 times in LXX, 22 times in N.T.).

τί ἐξουδενεῖς τὸν ἀδελφόν σου; gains force from a reference to the maxim, μὴ καταφρονήσητε ἑνὸς τῶν μικρῶν τούτων— among whom the 'weak' brother might well be counted (Matt. xviii. 10). This maxim in turn occurs in a context which speaks of the extreme danger of 'scandalizing'[1] a little one (Matt. xviii. 6), and this is echoed in Paul's injunction not to place a σκάνδαλον in the way of the weak brother. Finally, the sequence of sayings about 'scandals' and 'little ones', in its Marcan form (Mk. ix. 33–50), ends with the saying, εἰρηνεύετε ἐν ἑαυτοῖς, which has an echo in Rom. xiv. 19, τὰ τῆς εἰρήνης διώκομεν (v.l. διώκωμεν) . . . τῆς εἰς ἀλλήλους.[2]

This discussion, therefore, is notably full of what appear to be reminiscences of sayings which at the time when the gospels were written formed part of the tradition accepted as the teaching of Jesus. The method which Paul is here following is fundamentally similar to that employed in I Cor. vii. 10–11, where he glosses and applies the ἐπιταγὴ Κυρίου, except that in Romans the basic maxims are not expressly cited but adduced allusively, and that the procedure is sustained over a long passage of casuistry. It is in fact not essentially different from the method by which in rabbinic writings *halakha* is based upon precepts cited from the Torah. In other words, maxims which formed part of the tradition of the sayings of Jesus are treated as if they were in some sort elements of a new Torah.

For our present purpose it is not without importance that the two places where Paul most distinctly cites sayings of the Lord as an authoritative basis for his own instructions to the Church occur in the same epistle to which our fundamental

---

[1] Σκανδαλίζειν in this sense is unknown to profane Greek. Σκανδαλιστής is some kind of public entertainer, an 'acrobat' (Liddell & Scott, *s.v.*) or 'Zauberkünstler' (Dittenberger, *Sylloge*[3] 847); σκάνδαλον is not attested outside biblical Greek. It is significant that in this short context Paul has used two un-Greek expressions which are firmly rooted in the tradition of the sayings of Jesus.

[2] See p. 26 above, where it is suggested that Paul's τὰ τῆς εἰρήνης διώκωμεν and Mark's εἰρηνεύετε ἐν ἀλλήλοις (as a comment on the *Bildwort* about salt) may both go back to the common *catechesis* of the primitive Church.

L

text belongs, and in fairly close juxtaposition to it. If in the seventh chapter of that epistle he speaks of an ἐπιταγὴ Κυρίου, and at an early point in the ninth chapter settles a controversial point with the words, ὁ Κύριος διέταξεν, and if then at a later point in the same chapter he uses the expression ἔννομος Χριστοῦ, it is reasonable to conclude that such ἐπιταγαί and διατάγματα are conceived as in some sort constituent elements in the 'law of Christ'.

Let us now turn once again to the one place where that expression, ὁ νόμος τοῦ Χριστοῦ, occurs (Gal. vi. 2). We return to it with a certain presumption that a reference is intended to something in the way of ἐπιταγαί or διατάγματα Κυρίου. At first sight it is not easy to identify here any maxim otherwise attested as belonging to the tradition of the Sayings. But the main theme of Gal. vi. 1–5 is that of the treatment of a Christian who falls into sin. Those members of the community who have gifts of the Spirit (πνευματικοί) are to restore him. In doing so they must show that gentleness (πραΰτης) which is a 'fruit of the Spirit', and recognize their own fallibility, since self-deception is all too easy. Thus they will help to bear one another's βάρη. At the same time each must remain aware of his own inalienable responsibility: he must bear his own φορτίον. Now in Matt. xxiii. 4 it is a count against the 'scribes and Pharisees' as teachers and pastors of their people that they lay upon them φορτία βαρέα which they themselves will not touch with their little finger. It would be a natural counterpart to this that the Christian πνευματικός should both carry his own φορτίον and help to carry the other man's βάρος. Again, the injunction about restoring the erring brother finds a parallel in the rudimentary 'church-order' of Matt. xviii. 15–20, which was certainly handed down as part of the teaching of Jesus. Paul is applying the precepts of Matt. xviii. 15–16, without going into the details of procedure. That he also observed the further precept governing cases where the attempt at restoration fails (xviii. 17) we know from I Cor. v. 4–5. These verses appear to reproduce the actual formula of excommunication, and the clause ἐν τῷ ὀνόματι τοῦ Κυρίου Ἰησοῦ συναχθέντων ὑμῶν echoes the Matthaean συνηγμένοι εἰς τὸ ἐμὸν ὄνομα (xviii. 20), which is here treated as covering the whole scheme of church discipline in 15–20. Whether it is the restoration of an offender, or the expulsion of the contumacious, or the establishment of rules of Christian living ('binding and loosing'),[1] the 'assembly in the name of the Lord Jesus' is essential to give validity to the proceedings. It appears therefore that to 'fulfil the law of Christ' means a good deal more than simply to act 'in a Christian spirit' (as we say). It connotes the intention to carry out—in a different setting and in altered circumstances, it is true—the precepts which Jesus Christ was believed to have given to his disciples, and which they handed down in the Church. This is to be ἔννομος Χριστοῦ.

From another point of view the restoration of the erring brother, the shouldering of personal responsibility, and the sharing of burdens, are cases of πνεύματι ἄγεσθαι, στοιχεῖν, περιπατεῖν. The apparent tension between two ways of regarding Christian behaviour is lessened if we no longer think (as too much modern interpretation of Paul has thought) of the Christian πνευματικός as a solitary individual taking his stand upon the guidance he receives from the Spirit as 'inner light', over against the tradition and authority of the community, and think of him rather as one who lives and moves within the Body which the Spirit inhabits. The Body is constituted by the act and word of Christ, proclaimed in the Gospel and witnessed by his apostles. Each member, by virtue of the κοινωνία τοῦ πνεύματος, is offered the guidance and help of the Spirit to understand the law of Christ, to apply it, to discern its relevance to fresh situations, and finally to fulfil it; but he is not promised (at least by Paul) independent knowledge of the law

---

[1] The authority to forbid (δῆσαι, אסר) or to permit (λῦσαι, שרא) certain forms of behaviour within the community is precisely the authority which Paul claims to have been committed to him by the Lord, εἰς οἰκοδομήν (II Cor. xiii. 10), as in Matt. xvi. 19 it is committed to Peter, in a maxim which falls under the governing conception οἰκοδομήσω μου τὴν ἐκκλησίαν.

Reflection upon this may throw light upon Paul's anxious insistence on his right to be considered an 'apostle' not inferior to Cephas (Gal. ii. 8, etc.).

of God, unrelated to the teaching which Jesus delivered to his people. The Spirit writes this teaching 'on his heart'.[1] Part of this process we may observe in such passages as Rom. xiv., I Cor. vii., viii.–ix., Gal. v. 25–vi. 5. But it is not suggested that the law originates in the inspiration of Christian 'prophets'. Certainly it would be a mistake to attempt to confine the connotation of ὁ νόμος τοῦ Χριστοῦ to the comparatively restricted body of traditional Sayings of Jesus, but it appears that even for Paul, with his strong sense of the immediate governance of Christ through his Spirit in the Church, that which the Lord 'commanded' and 'ordained' remains the solid, historical and creative nucleus of the whole.

[1] I have discussed the relation between the recorded teaching of Jesus and the law 'written on the heart' in *Gospel and Law*, pp. 64–83.

Index Nominum

Abraham, 4–46, 56
Abtinas, House of, 37
Alexander the Great, 64
Annas, 91, 99
Antiochus Epiphanes, 81–2
Aqiba (Rabbi), 4

Bacon, B. W., 81
Bauer, W., 48
Bédier, J., 1
Billerbeck, H. L., 37, 38, 54, 55, 56, 63, 92
Bultmann, R., 30, 31, 43, 54
Burney, C. F., 6

Cadbury, H. J., 124
Caiaphas, 59, 63, 65, 92, 99
Carrington, P., 11
Chadwick, H., 15
Chaytor, H. J., 1, 9
Claudius (Emperor), 141
Cleopas, 107
Creed, J. M., 109

Daube, D., 15
David (King), 76
De Vaux, R., 36, 38
Dibelius, M., 124
Dürr, L., 36, 37, 38

Elijah, 122

Festugière, A. J., 34, 35, 37

Gaius (Emperor), 81
Garmu, House of, 37
Gorion of Zaida (Rabbi), 37
Guria (Rabbi), 37

Heaton, E. W., 36
Hillel (Rabbi), 97, 138

Hisda (Rabbi), 38
Hyrcanus, 64, 65

Jaddua, 64
James (Bishop of Jerusalem), 43, 92, 114, 117, 125
Jeremias, J., 23, 29
John the Baptist, 52–4, 62
Judah ben Ilai (Rabbi), 37
Judas the Gaulonite, 79, 89

Kappara (Rabbi), 38
Klausner, J., 96
Knox, W. L., 21

Lietzmann, H., 25
Lightfoot, R. H., 122
Loisy, A., 45

Mara bar Sarapion, 85–6
Mary Magdalen, 110, 113–15, 129–130
Meir (Rabbi), 37
Milligan G.; see Moulton, J. H.
Mitton, C. L., 21
Moore, G. F., 36, 37
Moses, 97, 122
Moulton, J. H., 141

Nebuchadnezzar, 75, 76–7, 79

Pappos, 4
Paul, 47–52, 116, 122, 134–48
Peter, 43–4, 109, 116–7, 119
Philo (see also Index Locorum), 47
Phocylides (Pseudo-), 15
Pontius Pilate, 84, 88, 89, 101, 115
Pythagoras, 86

Rajna, P., 9
Robinson, J. A. T.; see Woolwich, Bishop of

Schlatter, A., 65
Selwyn, E. G., 12
Shammai (Rabbi), 97
Sherwin-White, A. N., 92
Silvanus, 13
Simon the Just, 65
Socrates, 86
Stephen, 92
Strack, P.; see Billerbeck, H. L.

Taylor, V., 59
Thomas (Apostle), 111, 115–16
Tiberius (Emperor), 84, 90
Titus (Emperor), 72, 79
Toynbee, A. J., 5

Wellhausen, J., 75
Wetstein, J. J., 48
Woolwich, Bishop of, 31

Index Locorum

Genesis
  iii. 16, 143
  iv. 21, 36
Exodus
  xii. 26–7, 36
Numbers
  xvi. 45, 77
Deuteronomy
  iv. 9–10, 36
  iv. 19, 68
  vi. 7, 20 sqq., 36
  viii. 11, 142
  xiii. 1–11, 84–5
  xiii. 7, 68
  xxi. 22, 84–5
  xxi. 23, 87
  xxviii. 64, 78
  xxx. 17, 68
  xxxii. 7, 46, 36
Joshua
  vii. 9, 77
I Samuel (I Kingdoms)
  x. 12, 35
  xxiii. 8, 77
II Samuel (II Kingdoms)
  ii. 12, 33
  xv. 14, 78
I Kings (III Kingdoms)
  xiii. 11–13, 35
II Kings (IV Kingdoms)
  ii. 3–7, 35
  ii. 11, 131
  ii. 12, 35
  vi. 14, 77
  viii. 12, 80
  xv. 16, 80
  xix. 4, 6, 22, 93
  xxv. 1–2, 77
I Chronicles
  iv. 14, 36
II Chronicles
  xxiv. 18, 78

Nehemiah
  iii. 8, 31, 36
Psalms
  i. 6
  ii. 1–2, 88
  xxviii (xxix) 3, 122
  xxx (xxxi) 14, 60
  xxxi (xxxii) 1–2, 6
  xl (xli) 2–3, 6
  xli. 3–4 (xlii. 2–3), 8
  lxiv (lxv.) 5, 6
  lxxvii (lxxviii) 21, 78
  lxxxiii (lxxxiv) 5–6, 6
  lxxxiii. 13 (lxxxiv. 12), 1, 6
  lxxxviii (lxxxix) 16–17, 6
  cxi (cxii), 6
  cxviii (cxix) 1–2, 6
  cxxvii (cxxviii) 1–4, 6
  cxxxvi (cxxxvii) 9, 75
  cxlv (cxlvi) 5–7, 6
Proverbs
  i. 8, 35
  ii. 1, 35
  iii. 1, 35
  iv. 10, 35
  xxxi. 1, 35
Ecclesiastes
  viii. 12–13, 4
  x. 16–17, 4
Isaiah
  iii. 25–6, 75
  xi. 12, 59
  xiv. 12–14, 82
  xxix. 3, 76
  xxxvii. 33, 76
  xliii. 5, 59
  lii. 5, 93
  liii. 11–12, 63
  lxiii. 16, 56
  lxvi. 3, 93
Jeremiah
  iv. 7, 73

Jeremiah—*contd.*
  vi. 15, 78
  vii. 11, 34, 73
  x. 15, 78
  xvi. 4, 78
  xx. 4–6, 78
  xxi. 7, 78
  xxii. 5, 73
  xxvi. 10, 21, 78
  xxvii. 27, 31, 78
  xxvii. 29, 77
  xxxii. 4 (xxv. 18), 73
  li (xliv) 6, 22, 73
  lii. 4–5, 76
Ezekiel
  iv. 1–3, 76
  xxi. 22 (27), 76
  xxvi. 8, 77
  xxviii. 25, 59
  xxxiv. 16, 89
Hosea
  ix. 7, 78
  x. 14, 75
  xiv. 1, 75, 80
Amos
  i. 3, 13, 80
  v. 18–19, 80
  vii. 14, 35
Nahum
  iii. 10, 75
Zephaniah
  i. 14–15, 78
Zechariah
  xii. 3, 78
Malachi
  ii. 10, 55

Tobit
  i. 10, 78
  xiii. 9, 8
  xiii. 12, 4
  xiii. 14, 4, 8
Ecclesiasticus (The Wisdom of
    Jesus Son of Sirach)
  ii. 1, 35
  xxiv. 21, 8

  xxv. 7–11, 7
  xxx. 1–3, 38
I Maccabees
  i. 54, 81
  ii. 28, 81–2
  ix. 62, 77
  xv. 13–14, 77
II Maccabees
  ix. 2, 77

Matthew
  iii. 2, 55
  iii. 7–10, 52
  iii. 7, 54
  iii. 9, 55
  v. 3–12, 1–2
  v. 3–16, 17
  v. 14, 27
  v. 16, 27, 28
  v. 17–48, 17
  vi. 1–18, 17, 22
  vi. 1, 27
  vii. 1–2, 144
  vii. 6, 17
  vii. 15–20, 17
  vii. 21, 52
  vii. 22, 17
  viii. 11–12, 55
  viii. 22, 56
  viii. 28–34, 103
  ix. 18–26, 103
  ix. 27–31, 104
  x. 18, 67
  x. 37, 56
  xi. 1, 141
  xi. 21–4, 97
  xii. 28, 8, 98
  xii. 33, 95
  xii. 43, 31
  xiii. 55, 37
  xiv. 28–31, 120
  xvi. 19, 147
  xviii. 6, 66, 145
  xviii. 10, 145
  xviii. 15–20, 106, 146
  xviii. 15, 134

xix. 4–9, 142
xx. 29–34, 104
xxiii. 4, 146
xxiii. 9, 55
xxiii. 23, 95
xxiii. 24, 31
xxiii. 33, 54
xxiv. 15, 80
xxiv. 43–4, 23
xxv. 13, 20
xxv. 31–4, 117
xxvi. 3–5, 59, 60
xxvi. 25, 90
xxvi. 59–66, 91
xxvi. 60–1, 97
xxvii. 20–2, 101
xxviii. 1, 127
xxviii. 8–10, 105–7
xxviii. 9–10, 127, 129
xxviii. 17–18, 105
xxviii. 19, 109, 131

Mark
i. 15, 54
i. 19–20, 37
ii. 3–12, 98
ii. 15–20, 59
ii. 24–8, 59
iii. 27, 31
iii. 31–5, 59
iv. 11, 27
iv. 21, 27, 31
iv. 22, 27
iv. 35, 41, 122–3
v. 1–43, 103
vi. 3, 37
vi. 14–29, 60–1
vi. 45–51, 119–21
vii. 13, 95
vii. 14–23, 25–6
vii. 18–19, 144
ix. 2–8, 121–2
ix. 33–50, 145
ix. 33–5, 59
ix. 42, 66
ix. 49–50, 26–7
x. 3–9, 142
x. 13–16, 59

x. 29, 56
x. 45, 62
xi. 17, 73
xi. 27–33, 100
xii. 13–17, 59
xiii. 5–27, 69
xiii. 9–10, 67
xiii. 13, 20
xiii. 14–20, 70, 71, 74, 80–3
xiii. 14, 80, 82
xiii. 15, 82
xiii. 17, 75
xiii. 22, 82
xiii. 29, 33, 37, 20
xiv. 1–2, 60
xiv. 10–11, 60
xiv. 38, 21
xiv. 48, 66
xiv. 53–64, 68
xiv. 55–64, 91
xiv. 57–9, 68, 97
xv. 9–13, 101
xvi. 9–11, 129
xvi. 10–11, 130
xvi. 12–13, 129, 130
xvi. 14–15, 110, 126, 128–9, 130
xvi. 15–16, 131
xvi. 19, 123

Luke
i. 53, 5
iii. 7–9, 52
iii. 13, 141
v. 1–11, 118–19
vi. 21–3, 2–6
vi. 40, 33, 34, 39
viii. 2, 130
viii. 16, 39
ix. 59, 56
x. 12–15, 97
xi. 20, 98
xi. 21–2, 40
xi. 33–5, 27
xi. 42, 95
xii. 22–46, 18
xii. 39, 23
xii. 47–8, 40
xii. 57, 66

Luke—*contd.*
  xiii. 31–3, 59
  xiv. 26, 56
  xiv. 34–5, 27
  xvi. 19–31, 5
  xvi. 24–5, 55
  xvii. 24, 31, 80
  xix. 42–4, 74–8
  xix. 46, 73
  xxi. 12, 67
  xxi. 19, 20
  xxi. 20–4, 71–4, 79
  xxi. 21, 78
  xxi. 25, 122
  xxi. 34–6, 20, 22
  xxii. 66–71, 91
  xxiv. 11, 130
  xxiv. 13–35, 107–8
  xxiv. 21, 126
  xxiv. 33–4, 127
  xxiv. 36–49, 110–13, 116
  xxiv. 36–43, 126
  xxiv. 51, 123
John
  i. 13, 53
  ii. 19, 68, 97
  iii. 25–30, 61–2
  iii. 29, 30
  iv. 28–9, 61
  iv. 41–2, 61
  v. 19–30, 31–2, 98
  v. 19–20, 31–2, 38–9
  vi 15–16, 121
  vi. 15, 100
  vi. 16–21, 119–21
  vi. 46, 39
  vii. 12, 89
  vii. 40–52, 61
  vii. 49, 95
  viii. 31–58, 41–57
  viii. 33, 48, 53
  viii. 34, 49
  viii. 35, 30, 47
  viii. 38–9, 50–1
  viii. 39–41, 47
  viii. 41, 55
  viii. 43, 51

  viii. 44, 49
  viii. 45–7, 51
  viii. 59, 88
  ix. 13–34, 61
  x. 1–5, 31
  x. 15–16, 58
  x. 22–38, 98
  xi. 1–44, 58
  xi. 47–53, 58–68, 91
  xii. 23–33, 58
  xii. 32, 58
  xii. 35, 30
  xii. 50, 143
  xiv. 16–19, 127
  xiv. 18, 118
  xvi. 2, 67
  xviii. 13, 67
  xviii. 19–23, 68
  xviii. 19, 91
  xviii. 31, 92
  xviii. 33–8, 90
  xix. 14, 68
  xx. 11–17, 110, 113–15
  xx. 19–21, 126
  xx. 20–1, 105–6, 109
  xx. 26–9, 110, 115–16
  xxi. 1–14, 107–9
  xxi. 7, 120
Acts
  i. 3–4, 123–4
  i. 9–11, 123
  i. 9, 131
  ii. 23, 135
  ii. 36, 87
  iv. 10, 87
  iv. 26, 87
  v. 30, 86
  vi–vii, 92
  vii. 44, 141
  x. 34–43, 124
  x. 39, 86
  x. 45, 43
  xi. 2, 43, 44
  xv. 5, 44
  xv. 45, 43
  xviii. 2, 141
  xxi. 20, 43

xxi. 23, 66
xxiii. 27, 77
xxiii. 31, 141
xxiv. 23, 141
Romans
  i. 29–31, 24–5
  iv. 14, 46
  iv. 16–25, 49
  iv. 17, 53
  vi. 6–18, 49
  vi. 17, 13
  vii. 7–viii. 10, 136
  viii. 2, 139
  viii. 14, 140
  xi. 25–6, 79
  xii–xiii. 13–14
  xii. 12, 21
  xii. 17, 28
  xii. 18, 26
  xiii. 11, 18
  xiii. 12, 19
  xiv. 1–23, 144, 148
  xiv. 14, 25, 94
  xiv. 19, 26, 145
I Corinthians
  ii. 8, 87
  ii. 15–16, 140
  v. 4–5, 146
  v. 11, 24
  vi. 9–10, 24
  vii, 148
  vii. 17, 141
  vii. 25, 40, 142
  viii–ix, 148
  viii. 9–13, 134
  ix. 1, 25
  ix. 14, 141
  ix. 19–22, 134–48
  ix. 20–1, 137, 139
  ix. 20, 138
  xi, 23, 144
  xiv. 34, 143
  xiv. 37, 142–3
  xv. 1, 125
  xv. 3–8, 124–7, 129
  xv. 3, 125
  xv. 4–5, 126

xvi. 1, 141
II Corinthians
  iii. 6, 139
  iii. 17, 127, 139
  xiii. 10, 147
  xiii. 11, 26
Galatians
  i. 6–9, 45
  ii. 8, 147
  ii. 12–13, 44
  ii. 15–16, 21, 46
  iii. 7–29, 49
  iii. 7–18, 47
  iii. 16–17, 49
  iii. 26–7, 47
  iii. 27–8, 51
  iii. 29, 47
  iv. 1–10, 47
  iv. 5, 50
  iv. 6, 51
  iv. 21–31, 47–8
  iv. 29, 53
  v. 1, 47, 48
  v. 2, 46
  v. 13–23, 138–9
  v. 14, 47
  v. 18, 140
  v. 19–21, 24
  v. 25, 139
  v. 25–vi. 5, 148
  v. 25, 138, 139
  vi. 1–5, 146
  vi. 2, 137, 139, 140, 146
Ephesians
  v. 3–5, 24–5
  vi. 10–17, 14, 19
  vi. 18, 20
Colossians
  iii. 5–8, 25
  iv. 2–3, 19
  iv. 6, 26
  iv. 11, 44
I Thessalonians
  i. 9–10, 12, 12
  ii. 15, 25, 144
  iv. 1–8, 12
  iv. 3–9, 12–14

I Thessalonians—*contd.*
   iv. 9, 24
   iv. 11, 12
   iv. 13, 14
   v. 1–10, 23
   v. 2, 12, 13, 18, 24
   v. 3, 20
   v. 7–9, 19
   v. 7, 20
   v. 12–22, 12, 26
   v. 15, 13
   v. 17, 21
II Thessalonians
   ii. 1, 59
   ii. 3–10, 13, 82
   ii. 15, 12
   iii. 6–12, 12
I Timothy
   i. 6–11, 45
   i. 9–10, 25
   i. 9, 135
II Timothy
   i. 10, 14–15, 45
   iii. 9, 45
Titus
   i. 10, 14–15, iii. 9, 45
Hebrews
   vi. 6. 47
   xii. 14, 26
James
   ii. 5, 5
   iv. 9, 5
   v. 1, 5
   v. 7–9, 14
   v. 8, 18–19
   v. 13–16, 14
I Peter
   ii. 12, 15, 28
   iii. 16, 28
   iv. 1, 19
   iv. 3–9, 14
   iv. 7, 18, 19, 20
   iv. 8–9, 14, 19
II Peter
   ii. 21, iii. 2, 143
I John
   i. 1–3, 127–8

II John
   9, 46
Revelation
   i. 10–18, 116
   i. 10–11, 121
   i. 16, 122
   ix. 16, 77
   xix. 14, 19, 77

Gospel According to the Hebrews,
   117
Gospel of Peter, 117
Didache
   i–vi, vii–xv, 14
   xvi, 15, 22
Apostolic Constitutions
   V. 4, 14, 90

Philo (ed. Cohn & Wendland)
   De Cherubim 17, 64
   De Vita Mosis II. 3, 64
   De Congressu 170, 64
   De specialibus legibus IV. 192, 63
   De Praemiis 536, 64
   Quod omnis probus liber sit, 48
   Legatio ad Gaium, 81
Josephus (ed. Naber)
   Antiquitates
   xi. 327 sqq., 64
   xiii. 299–300, 64
   xviii. 261–309, 81
   xx. 200, 92
   Bellum Judaicum
   iii. 351, 64
   iii. 352–3, 65
   iii. 399–408, 64
   v. 269, 76
   vi. 418, 74
Manual of Discipline
   (ed. Löhse 1964)
   i. 9–10, 96
Mishna
   Kiddushin 4.14, 38
   Pirqe Aboth 1.1, 97
   Sanhedrin 6.4, 85

Mishna—*contd.*
  Yoma 3.11, 37
Babylonian Talmud
  Berachoth
  16b, 56
  61b, 4
  63a, 38
  Sanhedrin, 43, 68, 84–5, 87, 88,
    98
  Yoma, 87a, 4
Palestinian Talmud
  Kiddushin, 61a, 37
Tosephta
  Sota 13.5–6, 65

Aeschylus. *Choephori 205*, 123
Aristotle
  Analytica Priora, 27, 123
  De Arte Poetica, 16, 108, 123
Corpus Hermeticum *vii 27*, 20
Epictetus. *Dissertationes* II. *i. 23*,
  49
Tacitus. *Annales* XV. *44*, 84
Papyri
  Egerton 2, 131
  Oxyrhynchus 37–8, 39, 267, 275,
    282, 285, 308, 310, 32
    724, 725, 1206, 33
Sylloge Inscriptionum Graecarum (ed.
  Dittenberger, 1917), *847*, 145